Lactose-Free

MORE THAN 100 DELICIOUS RECIPES
YOUR FAMILY WILL LOVE

LUCY KNOX & SARAH LOWMAN

A FIRESIDE BOOK
PUBLISHED BY SIMON & SCHUSTER
NEW YORK LONDON TORONTO SYDNEY SINGAPORE

Created and produced by:
Carroll & Brown Limited
20 Lonsdale Road
Queen's Park
London NW6 6RD

Managing Art Editor Adelle Morris
Editors Salima Hirani, Caroline Uzielli
Photographers Richard Kolker, David
Murray

FIRESIDE
Rockefeller Center
1230 Avenue of the Americas
New York, NY 10020

Printed and bound in Italy by LEGO.

10 9 8 7 6 5 4 3 2 1

Library of Congress Cataloging-in-Publication
Data
Knox, Lucy.
    Lactose free : more than 100 delicious
  recipes your family will love / Lucy Knox &
  Sarah Lowman.
      p. cm. — (Great healthy food)
    Includes index.
    1. Lactose intolerance—Diet therapy—
  Recipes. 2. Milk-free diet—Recipes.
  I. Lowman, Sarah. II. Title. III. Series.
  RC632.L33 K665 2000
  641.5'63—dc21   00-024510

ISBN 0-684-87258-7

Contents

Introduction

I've always loved food and cookery and, at the age of 25 I was a complete foodie—both my personal and professional lives (I was Cookery Editor of the British magazine *Woman & Home*) were largely about cooking, eating and entertaining. That was when I developed an intolerance to lactose.

Rather than deprive myself of tasty meals, I became determined to learn how to cook delicious dairy-free meals that my family would be happy to eat on a day-to-day basis, and that dinner guests would enjoy, hopefully without even noticing the lack of dairy produce. I rose to this irresistible challenge and set about experimenting with new ingredients and trying out new approaches to all my favorite recipes. A little imagination and effort brought many wonderful rewards. Before long, I had discovered hundreds of new and delicious recipes and adapted my old ones, and I had a whole new dairy-free diet that I could share with my family and friends. The recipes here are the fruits of my efforts which I hope you will enjoy, whether you or a family member is lactose-intolerant.

LACTOSE INTOLERANCE

Before my condition arose, I had always assumed that lactose intolerance was hereditary. This can be true, but in fact, it can also be triggered off at any stage of your life for a variety of reasons. In my case, I was struck down with salmonella poisoning from a bad egg (an occupational hazard!), which then sparked off the intolerance.

Lactose is a white crystalline sugar present in the milk of humans, cows, sheep and goats. Intolerance is caused when there are insufficient amounts of an enzyme called lactase in the small intestine which allows your body to digest lactose efficiently. If lactose is not digested properly, it causes very painful gastric symptoms. The only cure is, initially, to cut out all dairy produce from your diet in order to allow your body to recover fully. The good news is that after a sufficient rest period of about a month or so, many sufferers can once again enjoy a limited amount of dairy produce. Doctors advise a slow reintroduction of lactose into the diet, starting with those foods which contain low levels of lactose, such as breads, cereals, fermented yogurt and hard cheeses. Some people find that after this initial rest period and gradual reintroduction of such foods, their bodies are even able to cope with a little bit of milk.

Recent research shows that it is far better to slowly reintroduce dairy produce into the diet than to eliminate it for good, which risks the development of other problems caused by a low calcium intake. Nevertheless, your body may never tolerate the levels of dairy foods that it once did. Therefore, it is necessary—and vital to your health—to keep to a predominantly lactose-free diet, so this book should be helpful for many years to come!

FOODS TO EAT FREELY

Build your diet around the following items:

All fresh vegetables—especially green vegetables which contain calcium.

All fruits—fresh and dried.

Seafood, poultry and lean meats.

Pasta, potatoes, rice.

Legumes and nuts.

Breads and cereals—some breads, including French, Italian, pita, rye, bagels, shredded wheat, rolled oats.

Milk-free substitutes—coconut milk, soy, and tofu-based cheese, yogurt, milk, and margarine.

Soups—broth-based and bouillon

Condiments—including mustard mayonnaise, ketchup, jellies and preserves, and honey.

Candy—bittersweet chocolate, marshmallows, licorice and fruit candies.

FOODS TO WATCH OUT FOR

These items may contain lactose:

Baked goods—croissants, breads, muffins, cakes, biscuits, pastry (not filo), doughnuts, crackers.

Sauces often based on butter and milk, such as white sauce and custard.

Soups—many are milk-based.

Processed foods—meats such as salami often contain lactose.

Egg dishes—pancakes and omelettes (often contain cheese).

Miscellaneous—salad dressings, milk chocolate (bittersweet is fine), ice cream.

Medicines, prescriptions and vitamin supplements—often listed as "sugar" on the packet which could refer to lactose.

FOODS TO AVOID

Milk—all types, including condensed, evaporated, goat's and sheep's milk and buttermilk.

Butter/margarine—all types.

Cheese—all types, including cream cheese and cottage cheese.

Cream and yogurt—all types.

Milk proteins (on ingredients list)—whey, lactoglobulin, casein, lactalbumin, sodium caseinate.

NUTRITIONAL KNOW HOW

Cutting out dairy produce eliminates the main sources of calcium and vitamin D. It is, therefore, vital to consume other calcium-rich foods as well as the recommended daily allowances of vitamins A, C and D, phosphorus, magnesium and potassium, all of which aid the absorption of calcium. Plenty of exercise along with a generally healthy lifestyle are also beneficial.

Calcium—canned salmon, mackerel and sardines, tofu, shrimp, kale, spinach, brussels sprouts and broccoli.

Vitamin A—carrots, spinach, beans, broccoli, sweet potatoes, peaches and dried apricots.

Vitamin C—citrus fruits, broccoli.

Vitamin D—added to milk products such as margarine, and produced in the body when exposed to sunlight, so unless you spend plenty of time outdoors it may be necessary to take a supplement such as cod liver oil.

Phosphorus—nuts, sardines, eggs, chicken, meat and red beans.

Magnesium—nuts, red and white beans, brewer's yeast and shredded wheat.

Potassium—dried fruits, nuts, avocados, bananas, scallops, chicken, beef and liver.

THE LACTOSE-FREE DIET

As you will see from the recipes in this book, fresh ingredients are the basis of a dairy-free diet. Over the years, I have learned to adapt my shopping and cooking habits to suit a diet that eliminates dairy products. For example, preparing delicious meals with sauces became far easier once I discovered the endless uses of the humble tomato. I now use a variety of simple and tasty tomato-based sauces in place of those based on cream, milk or cheese. Pastry needn't be a problem either, as it can be made easily using oil. Filo pastry (often found in gourmet stores) is a particularly good dairy-free ingredient for both sweet and savory dishes. Alternatively, a scone-based dough can be used in place of pastry as a substantial topping for pies.

When it comes to desserts, it may at first seem that a lactose-free diet prohibits all the tastiest foods, but this is untrue. Many dairy-free products that are available in health food stores and supermarkets provide delicious alternatives. You can also find ways of cheating; passing up ice cream became very easy for me once I discovered that I could make equally delicious (and healthier) non-dairy ice cream using coconut milk or oat drink, for example. Lactose-free iced desserts and yogurts are also readily available, taste wonderful and are a lot less fattening than their dairy counterparts.

Dairy products are often added to many ready-made products, so when shopping for your ingredients, make sure you check the labels carefully. If the goods are sold unpackaged don't be afraid to ask the staff for assistance. Bread is a particularly easy product to slip up on, because some bakers use a mixture of milk and water. However, if finding dairy-free bread becomes a problem, why not try making your own bread—the last chapter of this book contains three excellent recipes.

FOR THE KIDS

Unfortunately, many lactose-intolerant sufferers are very young, so I have devoted Chapter 5 to children's meals. Knowing how difficult they can be about food (I have two young daughters of my own), I have included plenty of tasty dishes, such as Pork & Apple Burgers (see page 88) which are lactose-free, but will not make your child feel that he or she is missing out on normal and fun kids' foods. However, before eliminating dairy produce from your child's diet, it is very important to get a proper diagnosis from a doctor or nutritionist as they will be able to monitor the calcium intake, which is a vital element in the diet of a growing body.

I would like to dedicate this book to my parents, Peter and Gina, and to my very dear friend Sarah Lowman, all of whom nursed me day and night during my salmonella scare, when I thought I was going to die, and when, quite frankly, I was not a pleasant person to know. Sarah also proved to be a great source of inspiration and support when I was looking for delicious ways around my lactose intolerance. I would also like to dedicate this book to my husband, Keith Richmond, for picking up the pieces after my illness.

1

Soups & Appetizers

FRENCH ONION SOUP WITH SUN-DRIED TOMATO TOPPING

3 tablespoons olive oil

1½ pounds onions, peeled and finely sliced

2 teaspoons sugar

¼ cup all-purpose flour

1¾ cups game, beef or vegetable stock (see page 77)

Salt and black pepper to taste

Small French baguette, sliced

4 tablespoons sun-dried tomato paste

2 cloves garlic, peeled and finely chopped

Serves 4

This traditional soup is given a unique modern twist by replacing the cheese topping with a crispy toasted topping flavored with sun-dried tomato paste. To caramelize the onions, use good quality olive oil and a generous pinch of sugar as substitutes for butter.

1 Heat the oil in a large heavy-based pan and add the onions and sugar. Cook over very low heat for 10 minutes until the onions are soft and just beginning to brown. Remove from the heat and stir in the flour.

2 Add enough cold water to the stock to increase the liquid volume to 3⅔ cups. Gradually add the liquid to the pan, stirring constantly. Return the pan to the heat and bring to a boil. Reduce the heat and simmer for 15 minutes, stirring frequently. Season with salt and black pepper.

3 Toast the bread on one side under a preheated broiler. Then, turn over and spread thinly with the sun-dried tomato paste and sprinkle with the garlic.

4 Ladle the soup into 4 ovenproof bowls. To serve, top each portion with a couple of slices of French bread, tomato paste-side up and place under a preheated broiler for 2–3 minutes until the bread is lightly toasted.

MIXED BEAN SOUP

3 tablespoons olive oil

2 medium-sized leeks, chopped

1 red bell pepper, deseeded and finely chopped

1 stalk lemon grass, bruised and finely chopped

2 cloves garlic, peeled and chopped

3⅔ cups vegetable stock (see page 77)

15-ounce can each pinto beans and navy beans, rinsed and drained

3 tablespoons shredded fresh basil leaves

Salt and black pepper to taste

Pimento paste to garnish (see page 31)

Serves 4–6

This delicious and fairly substantial soup is quick to prepare and is not puréed, so you do not need to own a food processor. It is wonderful accompanied with warm crusty bread rolls and garnished with a spoonful of pimento paste in the center of each serving.

1 Heat the oil in a large saucepan and add the finely chopped leeks, red bell pepper, lemon grass and garlic. Cook over low heat for 10 minutes until all the vegetables are slightly softened, but not browned.

2 Add the vegetable stock, stir well, then slowly bring to a boil over medium heat. Reduce the heat and simmer for approximately 10 minutes until all the vegetables are soft.

3 Add the rinsed and drained pinto and navy beans to the pan with the vegetables and continue to simmer for a further 5 minutes.

4 Stir the basil leaves into the soup and season with salt and plenty of black pepper to taste. Divide the soup between 4 serving bowls. Swirl the soup with a spoonful of pimento paste on to the top of each portion. Serve with warm crusty bread rolls.

BUTTERNUT SQUASH SOUP

Butternut squash has a brilliant orange color and subtle flavor that marries wonderfully with aromatic herbs such as coriander. This warming soup (see below) is served with home-made garlic croutons.

1   Heat ¼ cup of olive oil in a large saucepan and add the onions and 3 cloves of chopped garlic. Cook over medium heat for 5 minutes until the onions are softened. Add the squash, the sweet potato and the coriander and cook for a further 5 minutes.

2   Add the stock to the pan and bring slowly to a boil. Reduce the heat and simmer for 25 minutes until the squash is softened. Ladle the soup into a food processor (in batches if necessary) and blend until smooth or pass the ingredients through a sieve to purée. Season with salt and black pepper. Reheat the soup and serve with croutons.

3   Cut the bread into cubes. Heat the remaining oil in a skillet and add the bread. Cook over high heat for 5–10 minutes, turning the bread cubes frequently until crispy on all sides. Place them in a paper bag with the remaining garlic, seal the bag, then shake it vigorously to coat the croutons.

½ cup olive oil

2 medium-sized onions, peeled and chopped

4 cloves garlic, peeled and finely chopped

2 pounds (about 6 cups) butternut squash, peeled and diced

1 large (4–6 ounce) sweet potato, peeled and diced

2 teaspoons ground coriander

1 quart (4 cups) chicken or vegetable stock (see page 77)

Salt and black pepper to taste

4 slices bread, crusts removed

Serves 4

SALMON & SAFFRON RISOTTO

3 tablespoons olive oil

2 shallots, peeled and finely chopped

1¾ cups risotto rice

1 tablespoon saffron strands

1 quart (4 cups) hot vegetable stock
(see page 77)

¾ pound salmon fillet, skinned and boned

Salt and black pepper to taste

3 limes, cut into wedges to serve

Handful of fresh cilantro leaves
to garnish

Serves 6

Pink salmon and bright saffron bring vivid color to this dish
(see below). When making risotto either use Italian rice, such as
Arborio, or American medium-grain rice. Add a ladleful of stock and
wait for it to be completely absorbed by the rice before adding the next.

1 Heat the oil in a medium-sized saucepan and add the shallots. Cook
over medium heat for 5 minutes, stirring occasionally until they are
softened, but not browned.

2 Add the rice to the pan and stir to coat the rice grains in the oil. Add the
saffron and one ladleful of hot stock. Lower the heat and cook gently until
the rice has absorbed the stock. Continue adding more stock, a ladle at a
time, allowing the rice to absorb the liquid before adding the next ladle.
This should take 20 minutes.

3 Cut the salmon into bite-sized pieces and add these to the rice pan with
the last ladleful of hot stock. Heat the mixture for 3 minutes until the fish is
cooked through. Season with salt and black pepper and serve immediately,
garnished with lime wedges and cilantro leaves.

Lemon Thai Shrimp

The fashion for Thai food is extremely fortunate for those of us who suffer from a lactose intolerance as dairy produce plays a very minor part in Thai cuisine.

1 Shell the shrimp, leaving on the tails. Cut each shrimp along the center of the curve and remove the long black thread that runs along it. Rinse the shrimp under cold running water and pat them dry with a sheet of paper towel.

2 Place the lemon rind and juice, scallions, garlic, cilantro, chili and oil in a mixing bowl and stir until all the ingredients are combined. Season with salt and black pepper to taste. Stir the shrimp into this mixture, cover and leave to marinate for at least half an hour.

3 When ready to serve, preheat the broiler or light a grill. Thread the shrimp on to the lemon grass stalks and broil or grill for 4–5 minutes on each side until they become pink, turning and brushing with marinade as necessary.

4 To make the dip, mix the soy sauce with the red chili and cilantro. Place in individual bowls and serve with the skewered shrimp. Allow 3 skewers per person.

12–16 raw jumbo shrimp
(about ¾ pound)

Grated rind and juice of 1 lemon

2 scallions, sliced

2 cloves garlic, peeled and sliced

3 tablespoons chopped fresh cilantro

1 red chili, seeded and finely chopped

½ cup olive oil

Salt and black pepper to taste

6 stalks lemon grass, trimmed and halved

½ cup light soy sauce, 1 small
red chili, seeded and sliced and
1 tablespoon chopped fresh cilantro
for the dip

Serves 4

Golden Scallops with Spinach

Plump scallops are marinated in a mixture of exotic flavors, before being pan-fried and served on a bed of spinach.

1 Rinse the scallops under cold running water, drain and pat dry with paper towel. Place in a large bowl and set aside.

2 Stir together the orange rind and juice, cardamom pods, balsamic vinegar and 1½ tablespoons of olive oil in a separate bowl. Pour this mixture over the scallops and leave to marinate for at least half an hour.

3 Remove the scallops from the marinade using a slotted spoon. Place the remaining oil in a large skillet and leave over high heat until very hot. Add the scallops to the hot oil and cook them quickly over high heat for roughly 1–2 minutes on each side until golden and crispy on the outside but firm and juicy in the middle.

4 Divide the spinach between 6 plates and arrange the scallops on top. (The spinach does not need to be cooked as the heat from the scallops wilts the leaves.) Drizzle balsamic vinegar around the edge of each plate to serve.

18 fresh scallops, washed

Grated rind and juice of 1 orange

4 green cardamom pods, lightly crushed

1 tablespoon balsamic vinegar, plus
1–2 tablespoons extra for serving

3 tablespoons olive oil

¼ pound (about 4 cups) young spinach
leaves, trimmed

Serves 6

CHICKEN SATAY

Due to the increasing amount of alternatives to dairy products now available in large supermarkets and health food stores, cooking is far less limiting for those with an intolerance to lactose. This recipe uses soy yogurt, coconut cream and soy milk for a dairy-free version of chicken satay (see right).

FOR THE MARINADE

4 tablespoons plain soy yogurt

3 tablespoons crunchy peanut butter

Grated rind and juice of 1 lemon

3 tablespoons coarsely chopped fresh cilantro

FOR THE CHICKEN

4 boneless, skinless chicken breast halves (about 1½ pounds), cut into 4 thin strips

2 lemons, cut into wedges to serve

Chopped fresh cilantro to garnish

FOR THE PEANUT DIP

1 cup dairy-free coconut cream

4 tablespoons soy milk

6 tablespoons crunchy peanut butter

Serves 4

1 Soak 16 wooden skewers in cold water to prevent them from blackening under the broiler. Mix the yogurt, peanut butter, lemon rind and juice in a bowl. Stir in the cilantro and chicken breasts. When the chicken is evenly coated in the marinade, cover and chill in the refrigerator for 30 minutes.

2 Preheat the broiler. Thread one chicken piece lengthwise on to each of the skewers and arrange them on the broiler rack. Cook for 3 minutes until the chicken begins to brown. Turn the skewers over and cook for a further 3 minutes until the chicken is cooked through and evenly browned.

3 To make the peanut dip, gradually work the coconut cream and soy milk until a smooth paste is formed. Stir in the peanut butter and mix well. Serve the hot chicken satay with lemon wedges and the peanut dip. Garnish with a little cilantro.

TURKEY SATAY

Replace the chicken breasts with two skinless and boneless turkey breasts. Cut them into thin strips and follow the recipe as above.

PHEASANT WRAPPED IN PROSCIUTTO

Succulent pheasant breasts are wrapped in prosciutto, pan-fried and sliced thinly. They are served with a refreshing mixture of watercress leaves and orange slices.

4 pheasant breasts, skinned and boned

Salt and black pepper to taste

8 sage leaves

4 slices prosciutto

3 tablespoons olive oil

1 small bunch watercress and 2 large oranges to serve

Serves 4

1 Make a small pocket in the side of each pheasant breast using a sharp knife. Season inside each pocket with salt and black pepper and slip in 2 sage leaves. Then gently reseal by pressing the meat back together.

2 Wrap a slice of prosciutto around each breast. Heat the oil in a large skillet and add the wrapped pheasant breasts. Cook over medium heat for 8–10 minutes on each side until the prosciutto is crisp and the pheasant is cooked through.

3 Remove from the pan and slice the wrapped breasts thinly. Serve on individual plates with watercress leaves and peeled and sliced oranges.

TOASTED CIABATTA SANDWICHES

I ciabatta loaf or crusty Italian bread

I–2 tablespoons garlic oil

I tablespoon chopped fresh marjoram

Salt and black pepper to taste

2 medium red bell peppers, grilled (see below)

I baby eggplant, chargrilled (see below)

½ pound smoked ham, thinly sliced

Makes 2 sandwiches

Chargrilled peppers and eggplant in ciabatta make a tasty sandwich. For a vegetarian option, use fried mushrooms in place of the ham.

Slice the ciabatta loaf horizontally. Toast the cut sides under the broiler. Drizzle oil over the toasted sides and sit on a board. Seasoning each layer with marjoram, salt and pepper, place a layer of peppers on the bread, then eggplant, then one of ham. Press on the top half of the loaf and slice in half.

GRILLING VEGETABLES

Preheat a grill pan. Brush a little olive oil over thick slices of 1 seeded red bell pepper and 1 eggplant. Arrange on the pan and cook for 3 minutes on each side until the vegetables are softened and have grill marks on each side.

MINI PANCAKES WITH BRESAOLA & ARUGULA

I cup self-rising flour

½ teaspoon dry mustard

Pinch of salt

3 tablespoons rolled oats

I large egg, beaten

Approximately ⅔ cup oat milk

2 cups arugula, 6 ounces bresaola or smoked meat, sliced, and prepared chili sauce to serve

Serves 4–6

The peppery taste of arugula works well with bresaola (Italian dried beef) and a little chili sauce on these savory pancakes. For a vegetarian option, replace the meat with thinly sliced Italian or baby eggplant that has been browned in a tablespoonful of olive oil.

1 Sift the flour with the dry mustard and salt. Stir in the oats and beat in the egg. Add sufficient oat milk to produce a smooth, thick batter.

2 Lightly grease a griddle or skillet and place over high heat. Once hot, drop spoonfuls of batter on to the griddle and cook for 2 minutes on each side until golden. Cook the pancakes in batches and wrap in a warmed towel to keep warm. Serve topped with arugula, bresaola and chili sauce.

ROASTED VEGETABLE TARTS

FOR THE SCONE BASE

I¼ cups self-rising flour

I teaspoon dry mustard

2 large eggs

4 tablespoons olive oil

When I first learned I had a problem digesting dairy produce, I thought "How can I possibly live without pastry?" But I discovered that a scone base prepared with olive oil or oat milk makes a perfect replacement for pastry in many recipes. Here, it provides a good base for the smoky flavor of roasted vegetables in this colorful appetizer (see right).

1 Preheat oven to 220°C, gas mark 7. Slice off the tops of the peppers and discard, along with the seeds. Cut the flesh into 1-inch chunks.

2   Place the peppers in a large roasting tin with the onion wedges and halved
    garlic. Drizzle with olive oil and roast for 30 minutes, turning the
    vegetables once during cooking. Add the quartered tomatoes and roast for
    a further 15 minutes.

3   Meanwhile, prepare the scone base. Sift the flour with the dry mustard into
    a bowl and make a well in the center. Whisk the eggs with the olive oil and
    2 teaspoons of cold water. Place this in the well in the center of the flour
    and, using a fork, begin to incorporate the flour into the egg mixture until
    you have a soft, not sticky dough. Place the dough on a lightly floured
    surface and roll it out evenly. Cut the pastry into 6 rounds, wide enough to
    cover the bottom and sides of six 3-inch individual tartlet pans. Line the
    pans with the dough, doubling any overhanging dough back on to the
    sides and pressing the doubled dough to seal.

4   Divide the vegetables between the tartlet tins. Season with salt and black
    pepper and sprinkle liberally with thyme. Bake in the preheated oven for
    20 minutes. Serve Roasted Vegetable Tartlets warm with a salad.

FOR THE FILLING

4 medium-sized bell peppers, 2 red
and 2 yellow

1 large onion, peeled and cut
into 12 wedges

2 cloves garlic, peeled and halved

6 tablespoons olive oil

1 pound tomatoes, quartered and seeded

Salt and black pepper to taste

Fresh thyme to garnish

Serves 6

GOLDEN ASPARAGUS WITH LEMON PASTA

¾ pound asparagus spears, trimmed and halved

⅓ cup lemon oil

¾ pound fresh tagliolini or other thin fresh pasta

3 tablespoons coarsely chopped fresh tarragon

Salt and black pepper to taste

Serves 6

The best time to buy fresh asparagus is between February and June, although canned asparagus is always an option. Fresh spears should be prepared on the day of purchase. This recipe uses lemon oil which can be made at home—add the grated rind of 1 lemon to ¾ cup extra virgin olive oil and leave to infuse for at least 24 hours.

1 Heat a grill pan over medium heat. Arrange the asparagus spears on the pan and drizzle with 1½ tablespoons of lemon oil. Cook for roughly 3 minutes on each side, until golden and just cooked through.

2 Meanwhile, bring a large pan of lightly salted water to a boil. Add the pasta to the pan, return to a boil and cook for 2 minutes (or according to packet instructions). Drain and stir in the tarragon, cooked asparagus and remaining oil. Season with salt and black pepper and serve.

MIXED BEAN SALAD

1 cup each of cannellini beans, red kidney beans and navy beans

⅓ cup olive oil

4 teaspoons lemon juice

¼ cup chopped flat-leaf parsley

½ teaspoon superfine sugar

Salt and black pepper to taste

Serves 6

This attractive combination of beans is highly nutritious and can be altered to suit your taste by changing the variety of beans used.

1 Rinse and drain the cans of beans. Place them in a mixing bowl and stir to mix them together.

2 To make the dressing, blend together the olive oil, lemon juice, chopped flat-leaf parsley, superfine sugar and seasoning using a wire whisk. Make sure the ingredients are thoroughly blended.

3 Stir the dressing into the beans. Serve this salad immediately, or cover tightly and chill in the refrigerator for up to 2 hours.

GRILLED ENDIVE

¼ cup walnut oil

1½ tablespoons sherry vinegar

½ cup walnut pieces, coarsely chopped

¼ cup sunflower seeds

4 heads Belgium endive

Serves 4

Belgium endive is delicious when grilled—use red varieties, such as radicchio for this recipe, or try both for an attractive salad.

1 Preheat the broiler. To make the dressing, blend the walnut oil, vinegar, walnut pieces and sunflower seeds using a wire whisk.

2 Cut the endive in half, lengthwise, arrange on the broiler rack and drizzle a little dressing over them. Cook until they begin to brown around the edges. Remove from broiler, drizzle with the remaining dressing and serve.

CAESAR SALAD

Traditionally, Caesar Salad consists of salad greens and Parmesan cheese, which can be substituted with soy cheese for an excellent lactose-free version of this popular salad.

1 Separate the leaves from the lettuce heads, wash them, drain thoroughly and set aside. Crumble the soy cheese into a bowl.

2 Remove the crusts from the bread and discard. Cut the slices into small cubes. Heat the olive oil in a skillet over medium heat and add the crushed garlic. Cook for 1 minute, then add the cubed bread. Sauté the cubes of bread for 8 minutes, stirring frequently, until they are golden on all sides. Remove from the pan and drain the excess oil on a sheet of paper towel. Leave to cool.

3 Cook the eggs in a small saucepan of boiling water for 3 minutes until soft-boiled. Remove from the pan and plunge into cold water until cool enough to handle.

4 Shell the eggs and break them into a bowl. Using a wire whisk, gradually whisk in the oil, seasoning, lemon juice and Worcestershire sauce. Stir in the anchovies, if using.

5 Arrange the lettuce leaves and croutons in the bowl with the soy cheese. Pour over the dressing, toss gently and serve immediately.

FOR THE SALAD

2 small heads romaine

1½ ounces soy cheese (about ¼ cup once crumbled)

FOR THE CROUTONS

4 thick slices white bread

⅓ cup olive oil

3 cloves garlic, peeled and crushed

FOR THE DRESSING

2 large eggs

6 tablespoons olive oil

Salt and black pepper to taste

Juice of 1 lemon

1 teaspoon Worcestershire sauce

2 ounce can anchovies, drained and chopped (optional)

Serves 4

CHICKEN CAESAR SALAD

Sprinkle 2 chicken breasts, skinned and boned, with black pepper and lemon juice. Preheat the broiler and cook the chicken breasts for 5–10 minutes on each side until cooked through and browned on the outside. Cut the chicken into cubes or strips and use in place of the soy cheese in the Caesar Salad, above.

FOCACCIA CROUTONS

Focaccia can be used in place of the white bread in the Caesar Salad, above. Cut 4 slices of focaccia into cubes. Heat 1 teaspoon of chili oil and ¼ cup of olive oil in a skillet and add the focaccia cubes. Cook over high heat, turning frequently, for roughly 8 minutes until evenly browned.

Remove the focaccia from the pan and place immediately in a paper bag with 3 tablespoons of flat-leafed parsley, chopped. Seal the bag and shake well until each crouton is coated in parsley.

HERB & GARLIC CROUTONS

Either slices of focaccia or white bread can be used to make these herb and garlic croutons. Prepare the croutons as described in step 2 above, and place them in a paper bag with 2 peeled and crushed garlic cloves and 3 tablespoons of dried mixed herbs. Seal and shake the bag until each crouton is coated in the garlic and herbs.

2

Lunches
& Suppers

Fish
_____

Poultry
_____

Meat
_____

Vegetables

WARM MACKEREL & POTATO SALAD

½ pound new or small yukon gold or yellow finn potatoes, washed and halved

4 hearts romaine lettuce, washed and coarsely shredded

4 smoked and peppered mackerel fillets

4 sticks celery, cut into matchsticks

7 tablespoons light olive oil

Juice of 1 lime

1 teaspoon coarse-grain mustard

1 teaspoon honey

3 tablespoons snipped fresh chives

Crusty bread rolls to serve

Serves 6

This nutritious and satisfying salad takes only minutes to prepare, making it the ideal supper for the end of a long and hard day. Fresh sardines or anchovies can be used in place of the mackerel if you wish to vary the flavors.

1   Place the potatoes into a medium-sized saucepan of salted water and bring to a boil. Reduce the heat and simmer for approximately 15 minutes, until tender. Drain and set aside.

2   Meanwhile, arrange the washed and shredded lettuce leaves in a serving bowl. Coarsely flake the fish and add to the lettuce. Then add the celery matchsticks and toss the salad gently.

3   To make the dressing, blend together the olive oil, lime juice, mustard and honey using a wire whisk. (Alternatively, place the ingredients in a jar that has a lid and shake vigorously until the dressing ingredients are well combined.) Pour the dressing over the hot potatoes. Toss the potatoes to coat them thoroughly in the dressing.

4   Spoon the dressed potatoes into the center of the salad and garnish the dish liberally with snipped chives. Serve warm with crusty bread rolls.

PAN-FRIED MACKEREL WITH ORANGE & ROSEMARY

4 small whole mackerel, cleaned

2 oranges, halved and sliced

8 sprigs fresh rosemary

Salt and black pepper to taste

4 tablespoons olive oil

Green salad and crusty bread rolls to serve

Serves 4

Firm-fleshed mackerel has a delicious savory taste that works well with many flavors, making this a very versatile fish (see right). Traditionally, pan-fried mackerel is cooked in butter, but olive oil is a healthier and dairy-free alternative. When mixed with the sliced oranges and rosemary, you will find that it is just as tasty, too.

1   Rinse the mackerel and pat dry. Divide the sliced oranges and rosemary sprigs into four portions and place 1 portion inside the cavity of each fish. Season inside the cavities with salt and black pepper.

2   Heat the oil in a large skillet and arrange the mackerel so that they sit side-by-side inside the pan without overlapping (see right). Cook over medium heat for 3–4 minutes, then turn each fish carefully. Cook the other sides for 4–5 minutes until the flesh flakes easily and the skin is golden brown.

3   Remove the mackerel from the skillet and arrange one fish on each serving plate. Drizzle a little of the cooking juices on each mackerel and serve with a green salad and crusty bread rolls.

SMOKED COD WITH BACON

1¾ pound smoked cod fillets, skinned

8 slices bacon

¼ cup non-dairy soft margarine

1¾ pound potatoes (mashed with ¼ cup oat milk and 3 tablespoons olive oil)

¼ cup all-purpose flour

2 cups oat milk

3 tablespoons chopped fresh parsley

Salt and black pepper to taste

Serves 4

I was in a restaurant the first time I experienced the combination of smoked cod and bacon and I was amazed at just how well it works. Since then, this dish has become a firm favorite at home.

1 Cut the cod fillets into 4 equal portions. Wrap 1 slice of bacon around each piece of cod and dot with half of the margarine. Set the cod on a broiler and arrange the remaining bacon alongside. Broil for 2–3 minutes on each side, until the bacon is fairly crispy and the fish flakes easily.

2 Peel and wash the potatoes, cut them into small, even-sized chunks and place them in a large saucepan of boiling salted water. Return to a boil, reduce the heat and simmer for 10 minutes until the potatoes are soft. Drain, then mash the potatoes in the pan with the oat milk and olive oil until smooth. Cover with the pan lid to keep warm and set aside.

3 Place the remaining non-dairy margarine, flour and oat milk into a pan over medium heat. Increase the heat and stir the mixture constantly until it gradually comes to a boil. As it does so, it will become a smooth, thick sauce. Reduce the heat and simmer, still stirring, for 1 minute. Finally whisk in the parsley and season with salt and black pepper.

4 Slowly reheat the mashed potato, if necessary, adding more oat milk if it becomes too dry. Place a generous spoonful of hot mashed potato in the center of each serving plate. Set 1 piece of wrapped cod on top of each spoonful of potato and arrange a slice of crispy bacon on top of the fish. Spoon a little of the herb sauce around each helping using a small ladle. Serve the remaining sauce separately in a jug.

FLOUNDER WITH PEPPERS

6 tablespoons olive oil

2 medium-sized leeks, sliced

2 cloves garlic, peeled and thinly sliced

1 red and 1 yellow bell pepper, cored, halved and thinly sliced

3 plum tomatoes, skinned and coarsely chopped

Salt and black pepper to taste

4 flounder fillets, skinned

Serves 4

This colorful and simple dish is very easy to prepare. Serve it with warm crusty bread and a steamed green vegetable.

1 Heat 3 tablespoons of the oil in a saucepan and add the leeks and garlic. Cook gently for 5 minutes, then add the peppers and continue to cook for a further 5 minutes.

2 Stir in the tomatoes and cook until they have softened and most of the liquid has evaporated. Season with salt and black pepper.

3 Rinse the flounder fillets and pat dry. Heat the remaining oil in a skillet over medium heat then add the fish. Cook for 2–3 minutes on each side until just golden and cooked through. Serve the pan-fried flounder on warmed plates, covered generously with the sauce.

CRISPY HAKE & FRENCH FRIES

Hake is a low-fat fish with a white, delicately flavored meat that tastes great when battered. In this recipe I have used a light coating made from whisked egg whites, cornstarch and seasoning as a lactose-free alternative to batter.

1   Cut the hake fillet into 4 pieces. Mix the cornstarch, salt and black pepper in a bowl. Coat the fish pieces in the seasoned cornstarch and set aside. Lightly whisk the egg whites in a bowl, then dip the fish pieces into the whites to coat them evenly.

2   Heat the oil in a large, heavy-based skillet and add the fish. Cook over medium heat until the batter becomes crisp and golden and the fish is firm and cooked through.

3   Place the chilies, parsley, lemon rind and mayonnaise in a food processor and blend until combined. (Alternatively, crush the dry ingredients with a pestle and mortar and whisk into the mayonnaise.) Serve the hake with French fries (see page 84) and the chili mayonnaise.

1 pound hake fillet, skinned

6 tablespoons cornstarch

Salt and black pepper to taste

Whites of 2 eggs

3 tablespoons sunflower oil

2 red chilies, seeded and chopped

1 tablespoon chopped fresh parsley

Grated rind of 1 lemon

⅔ cup mayonnaise

1 recipe French fries (see page 84)

Serves 4

POTATO-TOPPED FISH PIE

A mixture of fish can be used in this delicious pie according to availability and also to suit your own taste.

1   Preheat the oven to 375°F, 190°C, gas mark 5. Place the haddock in a shallow pan and pour in the wine and ½ cup of cold water. Add the lemon, parsley and peppercorns. Bring to a boil, then simmer uncovered for 10 minutes. Scatter the shrimp into the pan and cook for 1–2 minutes until the fish flakes easily and the shrimp have turned pink. Drain the fish and reserve the cooking liquid. Skin and flake the fish and set aside.

2   Place the potatoes in a saucepan and cover with cold water. Bring the liquid to a boil, reduce the heat and simmer for 15 minutes until the potatoes are soft. Drain and mash the potatoes with the oil, then stir in the chopped parsley and seasoning.

3   Place the flour in a saucepan and gradually work in the reserved cooking liquid. Set the pan over low heat and stir until the mixtures has thickened. Season, then stir in the flaked fish and chopped eggs. Spoon the mixture into a large ovenproof dish.

4   Rinse and drain the spinach and place in a saucepan. Cook for 2–3 minutes until just wilted, then scatter over the fish mixture. Spoon the potato over the spinach and fork it into peaks. Bake for 15 minutes until piping hot.

1 pound haddock fillet

½ cup white wine

2 slices lemon

4 parsley sprigs

4 black peppercorns

½ pound shelled shrimp

2¼ pounds potatoes, peeled and chopped

3 tablespoons olive oil

3 tablespoons chopped fresh parsley

Salt and black pepper to taste

3 tablespoons all-purpose flour

4 large eggs, hard-boiled, peeled and coarsely chopped

¼ pound baby spinach leaves, trimmed

Serves 4

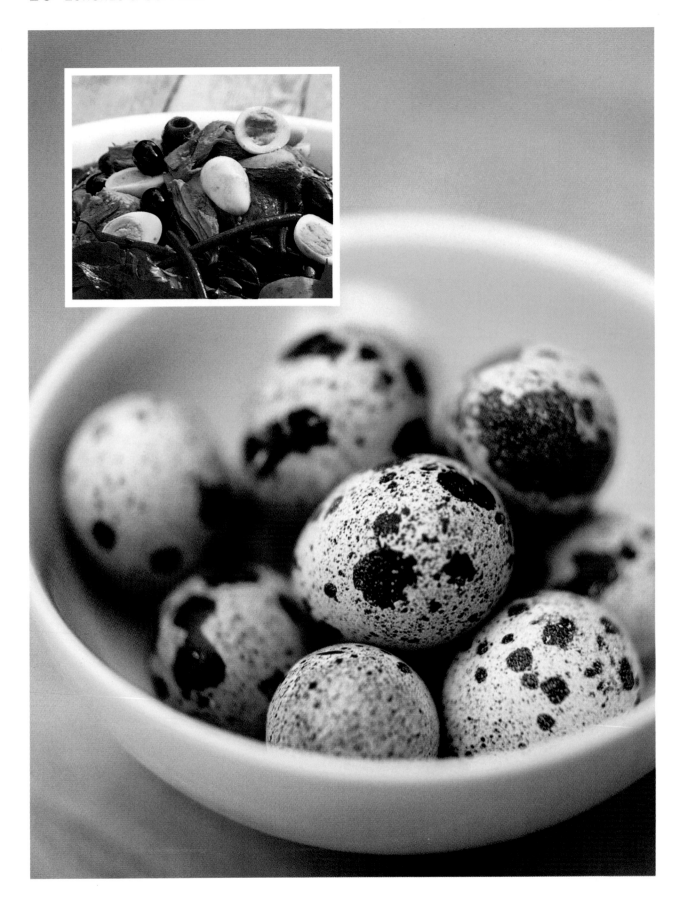

CLASSIC KEDGEREE

This Anglo-Indian dish, ideal for brunch, is also great for a relaxed supper with friends. Smoked haddock is my choice for this recipe, but as an alternative, try fresh or smoked salmon which are equally tasty.

Oil for greasing

1 pound smoked haddock fillet

1⅓ cups fish stock (see page 77)

1½ cups long-grain white rice, rinsed

½ teaspoon saffron strands

4 large eggs, hard-boiled and quartered

4 tablespoons plain soy yogurt

Salt and black pepper to taste

4 tablespoons chopped fresh cilantro to garnish

Serves 4

1 Preheat the oven to 400°F, 200°C, gas mark 6. Grease a 2 quart ovenproof dish with oil. Place the haddock in a skillet that has a lid and pour in the stock. Bring slowly to a boil. Reduce the heat and simmer covered for 8 minutes until the fish flakes easily. Remove the fish from the stock and allow to cool. Then remove the skin, coarsely flake the fish and set aside.

2 Add the rice with the saffron to a large pan of lightly salted boiling water. Bring back to a boil, then reduce the heat and simmer for 10 minutes, or according to packet instructions. Once cooked, drain the rice if necessary.

3 Spoon a layer of rice into the ovenproof dish. Add a layer of fish, then hard-boiled egg quarters and finally, dot with yogurt. Continue layering until all the ingredients are used up. Season each layer with salt and black pepper. Grease a sheet of aluminum foil with oil to cover the dish. Bake in the oven for 15–20 minutes until piping hot. Garnish with cilantro to serve.

SALAD NIÇOISE

There are as many versions of Salad Niçoise (see inset, left) as there are cooks in Provence—some dress it up while others dress it down. Usually it contains tomatoes, lettuce hearts, black olives, hard-boiled eggs, tuna and anchovies. Some cooks use quail's eggs (see left) or add pimentos and artichokes, while others like beans and new potatoes.

4 cups (about ¼ pound) mixed lettuce leaves, such as frisée, arugula and mâche

2 eggs (or 4 quail's eggs)

½ pound new potatoes

½ pound green beans, trimmed and halved

16 black olives, such as Calamata

2 x 6 ounce cans tuna chunks, drained

Rolled anchovies to garnish (optional)

FOR THE DRESSING

½ cup olive oil

3 tablespoons white wine vinegar

¼ teaspoon wholegrain mustard

1 tablespoon chopped fresh parsley

Salt and black pepper to taste

Serves 2

1 Wash and drain the salad leaves and set aside. Place the eggs into a small saucepan and cover with cold water. Bring to a boil and simmer for 10 minutes (3 minutes if using quail's eggs). Drain and cool under running cold water. Shell and quarter the eggs and set aside.

2 Wash the potatoes and cut any large ones in half. Cook them in boiling water for 15 minutes until tender, then set aside.

3 Blanch the beans in boiling water for 1 minute. Drain, refresh under cold water and drain again.

4 Place the lettuce on a large, flat serving platter. Arrange the hard-boiled eggs, blanched beans, potatoes, olives and tuna chunks on the lettuce.

5 Place all the ingredients for the dressing in a bowl and blend using a wire whisk until well combined. Pour the dressing over the salad, toss gently and serve with Herb Bread Rolls (see page 123) or crusty bread rolls.

HERB-COATED TURKEY

Turkey with breadcrumbs is a firm favorite in my family. For extra special results, take the time to marinate the turkey before coating it. Chicken breasts can substitute for turkey, but as these are smaller, use double the quantity.

FOR THE MARINADE

Grated rind and juice of 1 lemon

1 red chili, seeded and chopped

1-inch ginger root, peeled and sliced

Salt and black pepper to taste

2 skinless, boneless turkey breast halves

FOR THE TURKEY & COATING

2 cups fresh white breadcrumbs

2 tablespoons chopped fresh herbs, such as parsley, oregano and thyme

1 large egg, beaten

6 tablespoons honey

Serves 4

1 Mix together the lemon rind and juice, chili, ginger, salt and black pepper in a shallow dish. Cut the turkey breasts in half to make two cutlets and add to the dish. Stir the mixture to coat the turkey in the marinade, then cover and leave to stand for at least 1 hour, turning occasionally.

2 Mix the breadcrumbs and herbs together on a plate and season with salt and black pepper, if desired. Press each of the turkey pieces first into the beaten egg, then into the breadcrumbs so that both sides of the pieces are evenly coated in the batter.

3 Arrange the turkey pieces on a broiler rack or grill. Drizzle with half of the honey and cook for 10–15 minutes until golden. Turn each piece over, drizzle with the remaining honey and cook for a further 10–15 minutes until cooked through. Serve immediately with Seared New Potatoes (see page 65) and a simple green salad.

TOPPED BRUSCHETTA

The Italians originally developed this excellent way of making crisp and crunchy toast—sliced fresh bread is lightly brushed with oil that has been mixed with crushed garlic, then baked until crisp in a medium-hot oven. I like to make mine with a mix of olive and walnut oils. The toast stays crisp for roughly 12 hours, so this is the ideal dish for picnics—you can add the toppings when you get there. Serve the bruschetta (see right) with Mixed Bean Salad (see page 18).

FOR THE BRUSCHETTA

4 slices French bread

3 tablespoons olive oil

3 tablespoons walnut oil

1–2 cloves garlic, peeled and crushed (optional)

FOR THE VEGETABLE TOPPING

4 ounces artichokes hearts in oil, drained and halved

4 ounces roasted sweet red peppers in oil (about ½ small jar), drained and sliced into strips

Shredded fresh basil to garnish

Black pepper to taste

3 tablespoons olive oil for drizzling

1 Preheat the oven to 400°F, 200°C, gas mark 6. Arrange the slices of French bread side-by-side in a single layer in a large roasting pan.

2 Mix together the olive and walnut oils with the crushed garlic, if using. Brush half of the mixture on to one side of the bread slices. Bake the bread in the preheated oven for 8–10 minutes until crisp and golden, then turn the bread slices over and brush with the remaining oil. Bake for a further 8–10 minutes. Remove the bruschetta from the oven and allow to cool.

3 For the vegetable topping, arrange the strips of peppers and the artichoke halves on 2 slices of bruschetta. Garnish with basil and sprinkle with black pepper, then drizzle with olive oil directly before serving.

4 For the duck topping, arrange the sliced duck and tomatoes on top of the 2 remaining slices of bruschetta and garnish with thyme or arugula. Drizzle with olive oil and season with black pepper to serve.

PIMENTO AND PESTO PASTES

Either of these pastes may be spread on to slices of French bread in place of the walnut and olive oils and garlic mixture before being baked in the oven. Roasted vegetables are ideal as a topping for either pimento paste or pesto and the duck is particularly tasty with the pimento paste.

To prepare pimento paste, drain a 6½-ounce jar of pimentos and blend with 4–5 tablespoons of olive oil in a food processor. (Alternatively, crush the pimentos in a mortar with a pestle and mix in the oil.)

For pesto, blend ¼ cup pine nuts and 1 cup fresh basil leaves with ½ cup of extra virgin olive oil in a food processor. (Alternatively, crush the pine nuts and basil in a mortar with a pestle and gradually mix in the oil.) Season with salt and black pepper.

FOR THE DUCK TOPPING

I smoked duck breast, skinned and thinly sliced

4 red cherry tomatoes, halved

4 yellow cherry tomatoes, halved

Fresh thyme or arugula to garnish

3 tablespoons olive oil

Salt and black pepper to taste

Serves 2

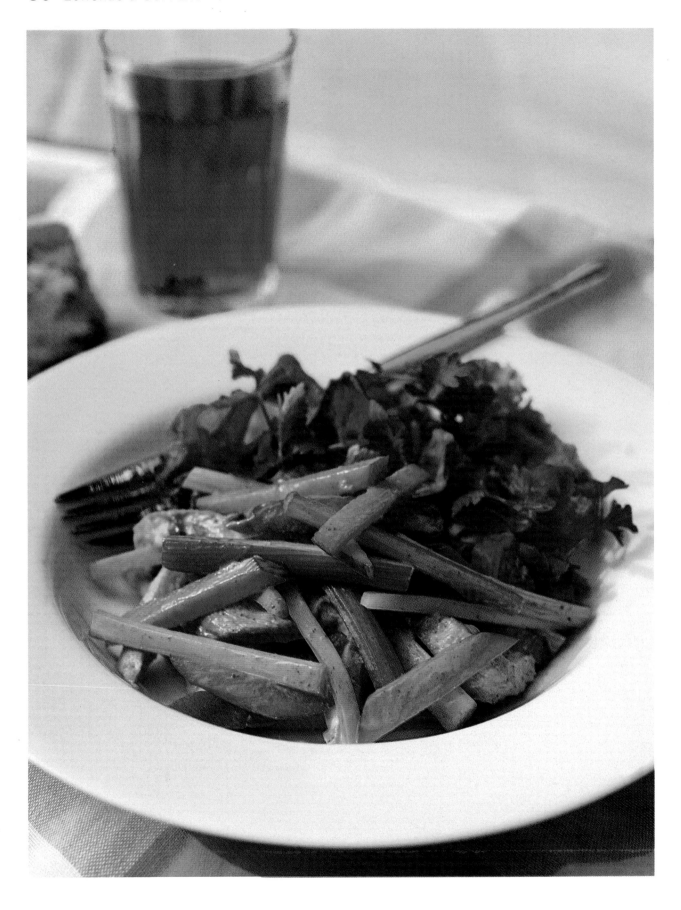

CRUNCHY CHICKEN SALAD

The crunchy vegetables and creamy, sweet sauce combine to create the perfect dish for a light lunch on a hot summer's day (see left).

1 Heat the oil in a skillet and add the onion. Cook over high heat until softened and beginning to color. Add the chicken and continue to cook over high heat for 10 minutes on each side until the chicken is golden and cooked through. Remove the chicken from the pan and allow to cool a little, then cut into fine strips and set aside.

2 Meanwhile, stir the curry paste and mango chutney into the pan with the onions. Cook gently for 5 minutes. Remove from the heat and allow to cool.

3 Mix together the peaches, celery, cooled curry mixture and mayonnaise, then stir in the chicken. Cover and chill for at least 30 minutes until ready to serve. Serve with Summer Flower Salad (see below).

3 tablespoons olive oil

1 onion, peeled and chopped

4 boneless, skinless chicken breast halves (about 1½ pounds)

3 tablespoons mild curry paste

3 tablespoons mango chutney

2 peaches, pitted and cut into matchsticks

1 head celery, rinsed and cut into matchsticks

⅔ cup mayonnaise

Serves 6

SUMMER FLOWER SALAD
Mix ½ cup edible flowers (such as nasturtiums, rose petals, borage or lavender) with 4 cups loosely packed salad leaves (mâche, arugula, frisée) and some fresh herbs (flat-leaf parsley, chervil, sage). Dress with an oil and vinegar dressing.

CHICKEN-STUFFED PITAS

Originally from around Greece and the Middle East, flat pita breads are traditionally slit open and stuffed. Here, they are given a fruity curried chicken filling.

1 Broil the chicken breasts under a preheated broiler for 5–10 minutes on each side until cooked through. Leave to cool, then cut the meat into cubes. Warm the pita breads in a moderate oven, then cut along half the circumference of each pita to open them out into "pockets."

2 Mix the scallions, the cooked, cubed chicken, the mango and grapes. Beat the mayonnaise in a separate bowl with the curry paste, cilantro, salt and pepper. Add the chicken mixture to the curried mayonnaise and stir to ensure all the ingredients are thoroughly coated in the sauce.

3 Coarsely shred the lettuces and arrange inside the four pitas. Spoon the chicken mixture into the pitas and serve.

2 boneless, skinless chicken breast halves (about ¾ pound)

4 white or wholewheat pita breads

2 scallions, trimmed and sliced

1 ripe mango, peeled, stoned and cubed

¾ cup halved seedless white grapes

⅓ cup mayonnaise

1½ tablespoons mild curry paste

3 tablespoons chopped fresh cilantro

Salt and black pepper to taste

2 medium heads romaine

Serves 4

DUCK AND VEGETARIAN STUFFED PITAS
Replace the chicken with two duck breasts, sautéed in the fat that exudes from the skin, for 6 minutes on each side. Or use 12 ounces cubed smoked tofu.

Chinese-style Pork

*One factor in favor of sesame oil is that a little of it goes a long way.
Another is its delicious nutty flavor which gives this stir-fry its
authentic Chinese taste.*

3 tablespoons light, untoasted sesame oil

¾ pound pork tenderloin
cut into thin strips

¼ pound sugar snap peas, trimmed

¼ pound broccoli florets

4 ounces (about 16 pieces) baby
corn, halved

1 red bell pepper, seeded and sliced

2 scallions, sliced

2 cups bean sprouts

1 teaspoon arrowroot

⅔ cup vegetable stock (see page 77)

1 teaspoon light soy sauce

Black pepper to taste

Serves 4

1   Heat the sesame oil in a wok or a large skillet. Add the pork and stir-fry over high heat for 5 minutes, until the pork begins to brown.

2   Add the sugar snap peas, broccoli, corn, bell pepper, scallions and bean sprouts and continue to stir-fry over high heat for 5–6 minutes, until the vegetables just begin to brown and wilt.

3   Blend together the arrowroot and stock and tip the mixture into the pan, stirring constantly to prevent lumps forming. Once the mixture thickens, remove from the heat and season with light soy sauce and black pepper. Serve with fresh rice noodles or plain boiled rice.

CHINESE-STYLE BEEF
Substitute thinly sliced top sirloin for the pork tenderloin. Stir-fry the sirloin for 1–3 minutes, add the vegetables and cook as above. Sprinkle liberally with toasted sesame seeds (cooked in a very hot skillet, shaking constantly until the seeds are golden) and serve with a little grated horseradish.

Spicy Beef

*To allow the flavors of the spicy beef fully to develop, it is a good
idea to prepare this dish in advance, cover it and leave it to stand for
24 hours. The egg topping can be made at the last minute.*

3 tablespoons olive oil

1 large onion, peeled and chopped

2 cloves garlic, peeled and chopped

3 tablespoons mild curry paste

1 pound lean ground beef

⅔ cup red wine

3 tablespoons chopped fresh cilantro

¼ cup slivered almonds

2 large eggs

1¼ cups plain soy yogurt

Salt and black pepper

Serves 4

1   Preheat the oven to 350°F, 180°C, gas mark 4 (if preparing and cooking on the same day). Heat the oil in a large pan and add the onion and garlic. Cook over medium heat for 5 minutes until the onions are translucent. Stir in the curry paste and beef. Increase the heat to high and cook until the beef is browned, stirring occasionally to ensure the mixture does not burn.

2   Add the wine and cilantro and cook for a further 2 minutes. Spoon the mixture into an ovenproof dish. At this stage, the dish can be covered and left in the refrigerator to stand for 24 hours, if desired.

3   Heat a heavy-based skillet until hot. Add the slivered almonds and cook over low heat for 1–2 minutes, stirring occasionally until the almonds are browned and toasted. Beat together the eggs and yogurt in a mixing bowl and season with salt and black pepper. Pour the egg mixture over the meat mixture and scatter the almonds on top. Bake in the preheated oven for 30 minutes until the "custard" topping is set and golden.

SAUSAGE & BEAN CASSEROLE

There is a wide variety of weird and wonderful sausages available, but I think one of the spicier varieties, such as the Spanish chorizo, is best for this rich and warming winter casserole.

1   Preheat the oven to 400°F, 200°C, gas mark 6. Place the halved bacon slices in a flameproof casserole that has a lid and cook gently until the fat begins to run. Increase the heat to a medium setting, add the leeks and cook until they soften. Add the salami and chorizo sausage to the casserole and continue to cook for 5 minutes until they begin to brown.

2   Stir the chopped tomatoes and beans into the casserole with the stock and bring to a boil. Reduce the heat and simmer for 15 minutes. Cover the casserole and cook in the preheated oven for 45 minutes.

3   Remove the casserole from the oven, season with salt and black pepper and stir in the parsley. Serve with baked potatoes.

14 ounces bacon slices, halved

2 leeks, trimmed and sliced

5 ounces salami, thickly sliced

6 chorizo sausages

28-ounce can chopped tomatoes

14-ounce can cannellini beans, rinsed

1⅓ cups chicken or vegetable stock (see page 77)

Salt and black pepper to taste

3 tablespoons chopped flat-leaf parsley

Serves 6

SEARED CALF'S LIVER WITH CRISPY BACON

½ pound (8–10 slices) bacon slices, chopped

1 tablespoon olive oil

2 onions, peeled and sliced

4 slices calf's liver, trimmed

1 tablespoon chopped fresh parsley

Black pepper to taste

Serves 4

Calf's liver is extremely nutritious, being rich in protein, iron and vitamin A, and it is packed full of flavor. The best way to cook it, in my opinion, is with bacon and plenty of fried onions...delicious!

1 Place the bacon in a skillet and cook over low heat until the fat begins to run. Increase the heat and fry for 10 minutes until crisp and brown. Remove the bacon from the pan using a slotted spoon and set aside.

2 Pour all but 1 tablespoon of bacon fat from the pan and add the oil. When hot, add the onions. Cook over medium heat until soft but not colored.

3 Arrange the liver on top of the onions and cook for 3–5 minutes on each side. Ensure you do not overcook the liver as it will become tough.

4 Return the bacon to the pan and mix with the liver and onions until heated through. Sprinkle with parsley and season with black pepper (there is no need to add salt as the bacon is sufficiently salty). Serve immediately with fresh peas and potatoes that have been mashed with olive oil and garlic.

LAMB WITH CRISPY POTATOES

FOR THE POTATOES

3 tablespoons olive oil

1 pound new potatoes, scrubbed

Large pinch coarse sea salt

4–5 sprigs fresh rosemary

FOR THE LAMB

8 small lamb noisettes

4 tablespoons mint jelly

FOR THE GRAVY

3 tablespoons all-purpose flour

1⅓ cups lamb stock or vegetable stock (see page 77)

Salt and black pepper to taste

Serves 4

Lamb noisettes (flattened, rounded pieces of lamb) are my first choice for this quick and simple supper dish, but if they prove hard to find, use lamb leg steaks instead which are readily available.

1 To prepare the potatoes, heat the oil over medium heat in a large saucepan that has a lid and add the new potatoes, sea salt and rosemary sprigs. Cover the pan and cook for 20 minutes, shaking the pan occasionally to prevent the potatoes from burning and sticking to the base of the pan.

2 Preheat the broiler. To prepare the lamb, brush each of the noisettes on one side using half the mint jelly. Broil the lamb, jelly-side up, for 2 minutes. Then turn the lamb over, brush with the remaining jelly and broil the other side for a further 2 minutes until cooked through. Remove the cooked lamb from the broiler and keep warm.

3 To make the gravy, add the flour to the lamb juices in the broiler pan and stir well. Gradually add the stock, then place the broiler pan on the stovetop. Cook for 3–5 minutes to thicken the gravy, stirring constantly to prevent lumps from forming. Season with salt and black pepper to taste.

4 Serve the lamb noisettes hot with the crispy potatoes, gravy and mixed stir-fried vegetables.

BACON & MUSHROOM OMELETTE

Omelettes are one of the easiest dishes to cook. The fillings can be as elaborate or basic as you wish. Here I have chosen a simple filling of slightly browned smoked bacon with shiitake mushrooms (that are cooked in the bacon fat) and garlic. For extra flavor, I like to add a variety of fresh herbs to the egg mixture.

1 Place the Canadian bacon or pancetta in a skillet and cook over low heat until the fat begins to run. Increase the heat and continue to cook for 3 minutes until the bacon begins to brown. Add the shiitake mushrooms and garlic and cook for a further 3 minutes, then set aside.

2 Lightly whisk the eggs in a bowl with 1 tablespoon of cold water. Add the chopped herbs and season with salt and black pepper.

3 Heat half the oil in a 8-inch omelette pan over medium heat and add half of the egg mixture. Tilt the pan or use a spatula to manipulate the egg mixture so it spreads to cover the base of the pan. Cook for 8–10 minutes.

4 Once the omelette is cooked, scatter half the bacon mixture over it. Fold the omelette in half while still in the pan and transfer to a warmed serving plate. Keep warm while making the second omelette using the remaining egg and bacon mixtures.

6 ounces Canadian bacon or pancetta, chopped

½ pound shiitake mushrooms, trimmed and quartered

2 cloves garlic, peeled and chopped

4 large eggs

3 tablespoons chopped fresh mixed herbs, such as parsley, tarragon or chives

Salt and black pepper to taste

1 tablespoon olive oil

Serves 2

PEPPER AND BEEF OMELETTE

Heat 1 tablespoon of sesame oil in a skillet and add 1 halved and thinly sliced red bell pepper and ½ pound of sliced lean beef sirloin. Cook over high heat for 5 minutes until the beef is seared (this process seals the meat's juices) and the pepper is just beginning to soften. Whisk the eggs with 1 tablespoon of cold water, 1 tablespoon of chopped fresh oregano and 1 teaspoon of prepared horseradish sauce. Cook as instructed above.

SMOKED SAUSAGE AND CARAMELIZED ONION OMELETTE

Heat 3 tablespoons of olive oil in a skillet and add 2 peeled and sliced onions and 2 teaspoons of granulated sugar. Cook over medium heat for 10 minutes, stirring frequently. Add 2 thickly sliced chorizo sausages to the pan and continue to cook for a further 5 minutes, until the onions have caramelized to a rich golden color and the sausages are heated through. Whisk the eggs with the water and cook as instructed above, adding the filling to the cooked omelettes before turning them on to warmed plates.

RATATOUILLE GRATIN

Traditional Provençal ratatouille is a combination of hearty vegetables that are cooked in olive oil, garlic and herbs. Here, I have topped this mixture with thinly sliced potatoes and soy cheese and baked the dish until the top is crispy and golden (see above).

| large eggplant, weighing approximately ¾ pound, sliced

1–2 tablespoons salt

½ cup olive oil

1 large onion, peeled and sliced

3 cloves garlic, peeled and chopped

4 ounces mushrooms, cleaned and sliced

1 pound zucchini, sliced

1½ pounds tomatoes, quartered

3 tablespoons each chopped fresh thyme and marjoram

Salt and black pepper to taste

1 pound potatoes, peeled and sliced

¼ cup freshly grated soy cheese

5–6 sprigs fresh rosemary

Serves 6

1   Place the eggplant slices in a colander and sprinkle with the salt. Leave to stand for 10 minutes to draw out the bitter juices. Rinse the eggplant thoroughly with cold water and pat dry with paper towel.

2   Preheat the oven to 425°F, 220°C, gas mark 7. Heat 6 tablespoons of the oil in a large skillet and add the onion and garlic. Cook over high heat for 5 minutes until softened but not browned. Add the eggplant, mushrooms and zucchini and stir-fry for 5–8 minutes until they start to wilt.

3   Stir in the quartered tomatoes and herbs and cook for a further 5 minutes. Season the mixture with salt and black pepper and spoon it into a large ovenproof dish.

4   Arrange the potato slices over the vegetable mixture so that they overlap. Sprinkle with the grated soy cheese and drizzle with the remaining 2 tablespoons of oil. Scatter sprigs of rosemary over the top.

5   Bake in the preheated oven for 20 minutes until the top is crisp and golden and the ratatouille is bubbling. Serve immediately on its own as a main course or as a side dish with roast lamb.

TABBOULEH

Bulgur wheat, which is available from most good supermarkets and at health food stores, is the main ingredient of this famous Middle Eastern salad. Chopped onions, tomatoes and a selection of herbs are also included, and I like to add meat or fish and grilled vegetables to make the dish less of a side dish and more of a meal-in-one.

1 Tip the bulgur wheat into a large heatproof bowl and pour in enough boiling water to cover. Leave to stand for 10 minutes until all the water has been absorbed by the wheat.

2 Coarsely chop the artichoke hearts and eggplant and place them in a large bowl with the ham, pepper and tomatoes. Mix thoroughly.

3 Run a fork through the bulgur wheat several times to separate the grains. Stir the ham and vegetable mixture into the bulgur wheat using a fork, then add the herbs, olive oil and lemon juice. Season with salt and black pepper and mix thoroughly. Serve immediately with a tossed green salad and crusty bread rolls.

2 cups bulgur wheat

6.5 ounce jar marinated artichoke hearts

7 ounces eggplant, chargrilled

½ pound cooked ham, diced

1 large bell pepper, chargrilled (see page 18) cut into strips

¼ pound tomatoes, cut into sixths

¼ cup chopped fresh Mediterranean herbs, such as basil, oregano and flat-leaf parsley

3 tablespoons olive oil

1 tablespoon lemon juice

Salt and black pepper to taste

Serves 6

SPINACH & POTATO CURRY

Fragrant spices such as turmeric, coriander, cumin and garam masala (a combination of roasted spices) marry wonderfully with the flavors of the potatoes, spinach and peas in this nutritious vegetarian meal.

1 Heat the oil in a large saucepan, then add the turmeric, garam masala and the coriander and cumin seeds. Cook the spices over medium heat for approximately 1 minute, stirring constantly until the spices are well blended with the oil.

2 Stir in the chopped onion and garlic and cook for a further 3–4 minutes. Then add the cubed potatoes and cook for another 3 minutes, stirring constantly until the potatoes are well coated in the oil and spices and just beginning to soften.

3 Pour the vegetable stock into the pan, then stir in the fresh peas. Bring the mixture to a boil, reduce the heat and simmer uncovered for 5 minutes.

4 When the stock has reduced and the potatoes are almost cooked, add the spinach and cook for roughly 3 minutes until it has wilted.

5 Stir in the fresh cilantro and season with salt and black pepper. Serve the dish either on its own with warm naan bread or as an accompaniment to a meat curry.

3 tablespoons sunflower oil

1 teaspoon turmeric

½ teaspoon each of garam masala, ground coriander and cumin seeds

1 onion, peeled and finely chopped

2 cloves garlic, peeled and chopped

1 pound potatoes, peeled and cubed

1⅓ cups vegetable stock (see page 77)

½ pound (about ¾ cup) fresh, shelled or frozen peas

½ pound (about 8 cups) loosely packed baby spinach, trimmed and halved

3 tablespoons chopped fresh cilantro

Salt and black pepper to taste

Serves 4

Mushroom & Prosciutto Pizza

It is no longer odd (in fact it is rather fashionable) to have pizzas without cheese on top—they can be just as filling and just as tasty. I like to top them with plenty of tomatoes, onions, mixed mushrooms and prosciutto. To complete, add your favorite herbs; arugula and flat-leaf parsley are particularly good (see right).

FOR THE BASE

1¼ cups self-rising flour

1 teaspoon dry mustard

3 tablespoons chopped fresh herbs

Salt and black pepper to taste

2 large eggs

4 tablespoons olive oil

FOR THE TOPPING

3 beef steak tomatoes, sliced

1 tablespoon olive oil

1 red onion, peeled and sliced

2 cloves garlic, peeled and sliced

½ pound mixed mushrooms such as oyster, cremini and shiitake, sliced

3 ounces prosciutto, cut into 1-inch strips

1 cup flat-leaf parsley or arugula

Black pepper to taste

Serves 4

1 Preheat the oven to 400°F, 200°C, gas mark 6. To make the base, sift the flour into a bowl with the dry mustard and herbs. Season with salt and pepper and make a well in the center of the mixture. Whisk together the eggs, olive oil and 2 teaspoons of cold water. Place the liquid in the well in the center of the flour and mix the flour into it a little at a time, until a soft, not sticky, dough is formed. Roll out the dough on a lightly floured surface to a 9 x 7-inch rectangle. Transfer the pizza base to a baking sheet.

2 Arrange the sliced beef steak tomatoes on top of the pizza base. Heat the oil in a large skillet and add the onions and garlic. Cook over medium heat for 5 minutes until the onions are softened but not colored. Stir in the mushrooms and cook for a further 2–3 minutes. Then spoon the mushroom mixture over the tomatoes on the pizza base and arrange the strips of prosciutto on top.

3 Bake the pizza in the preheated oven for 20 minutes, until the base is cooked and golden around the edges and the topping is piping hot.

4 Remove the pizza from the oven and immediately top with flat-leaf parsley or arugula. Season with black pepper. Serve drizzled with a little more olive oil, if desired, and a fresh green salad.

Chunky Spanish Omelette

Traditionally a Spanish dish, this chunky omelette is also known as a Tortilla and is usually served either warm or cold as a light lunch or as part of "tapas" (a selection of savory nibbles) with a glass of chilled medium-dry sherry.

6 tablespoons olive oil

¾ pound cooked potatoes, diced

1 leek, finely sliced

6 large eggs

Salt and black pepper to taste

¼ pound (about ⅜ cup) fresh, shelled or frozen peas

¼ pound (about 1 cup) broccoli florets

Serves 4

1 Heat the oil in a 9-inch non-stick skillet over medium heat, add the potatoes and leek and cook for 5 minutes until the leek is translucent.

2 Beat the eggs with the seasoning, then stir in the fried vegetables, peas and broccoli until they are all coated in the egg. Pour the mixture into the pan and cook over medium heat for 12–15 minutes until the top of the omelette begins to set and the bottom is cooked. Place the pan under a broiler and cook the top side of the omelette until set. Serve cut into wedges.

3 Entrées

FISH
_____

POULTRY
_____

MEAT
_____

VEGETABLES

HADDOCK WITH BEETS

FOR THE BEETS

1 pound, about 3 medium beets

Grated rind and juice of 1 orange

FOR THE FISH

4 haddock fillets (or turbot steaks), each weighing 6 ounces

Salt and black pepper to taste

3 tablespoons olive oil

3 tablespoons chopped fresh parsley

Serves 4

Haddock fillets are pan-fried in olive oil and parsley and served on a bed of thinly sliced beets which are flavored with a hint of orange. This dish shows that beets—often an underrated vegetable—can be an exciting and colorful addition to a meal. To vary the fish, use turbot steaks in place of haddock fillets.

1   To prepare the beets, peel and cut them into thin strips (julienne). Bring a saucepan of water to a boil and add 1 tablespoon of orange juice. Add the beets and cook for 5 minutes until they begin to soften. Drain and set aside.

2   Place the remaining orange juice and the rind in a skillet and cook over medium heat until bubbling. Then, add the beets and cook for a further 5 minutes, stirring frequently. Remove from the heat and set aside.

3   Season the fillets with salt and black pepper. Heat the oil in a skillet and add the fish. Cook over medium heat for 5 minutes, turning once, until the fish is golden and the flesh flakes easily. Divide the beets between 4 serving plates, place a haddock fillet on top and garnish with parsley.

SEARED TUNA WITH MIXED BEAN SALAD

FOR THE FISH

4 tuna steaks, each weighing ½ pound

Grated rind of 1 lemon

3 tablespoons chopped fresh parsley, chervil or dill

Salt and black pepper to taste

3 tablespoons olive oil

FOR THE SALAD

3 cups cooked mixed beans (such as red and white kidney beans and black beans)

1 red onion, peeled and chopped

⅓ cup Vinaigrette Dressing (see below, right)

Salt and black pepper to taste

Serves 4

Fresh tuna has a rich flavor and meaty texture. Here, it is cooked with simplicity in plenty of sizzling olive oil with a dash of lemon and a few chopped fresh herbs.

1   To prepare the tuna, rinse the steaks, pat dry and set aside. Mix together the lemon rind and your chosen herb in a bowl and season with salt and black pepper. Stir in the oil and mix until the ingredients are thoroughly blended. Spread half the lemon mixture on one side of the tuna steaks.

2   Arrange the steaks, lemon-side down, on a grill pan. Cook over high heat for 3 minutes, until golden. Spread the uncooked side of the tuna with the remaining lemon mixture, turn over and cook for a further 3 minutes.

3   Combine the mixed beans, chopped onion and Vinaigrette Dressing in a bowl. Season to taste. Divide the bean salad between 4 plates, place the tuna steaks on top and serve immediately.

VINAIGRETTE DRESSING

Place 6 tablespoons olive oil, 3 tablespoons lemon juice, 4 tablespoons chopped fresh parsley and half a teaspoon of superfine sugar in a bowl and whisk until all the ingredients are well blended. Season to taste with salt and black pepper.

WARM SCALLOP & AVOCADO SALAD

Scallops are easy to prepare and have a meaty texture and sweet, succulent flavor that is irresistible. Here, they are combined with crunchy walnuts, creamy avocados, fine beans and a tart lemon and mustard dressing (see below) in a salad that is perfect for relaxed summer meals with friends. This is the ideal dish for giving your guests an extra-special treat.

⅓ cup walnut oil

⅓ cup sunflower oil

1 pound cleaned scallops

¼ pound string beans, trimmed and cut into 1-inch pieces

2 ripe but firm avocados

¾ cup walnut halves

Juice of 1 small lemon

1 teaspoon wholegrain honey mustard

Salt and black pepper to taste

¼ pound (about 4 cups) loosely packed mixed salad leaves, washed

Serves 4

1   Heat the oils in a large skillet and add the scallops and string beans. Stir-fry over high heat for 5 minutes until the scallops brown on the outside but remain soft and juicy in the middle. Meanwhile, peel, stone and coarsely chop the avocados.

2   Add the chopped avocados and the walnuts to the pan. Continue to cook for 2 minutes, stirring frequently. Remove the pan from the heat and stir in the lemon juice and wholegrain mustard. Season to taste with salt and black pepper.

3   Divide the mixed salad leaves between 4 plates and arrange the scallop mixture on top. Serve immediately.

POACHED SALMON WITH FRESH HERB DRESSING

6 salmon cutlets, about 6 ounces each

1 bottle white wine

1 onion, peeled and quartered

2 sticks celery, roughly chopped

4 sprigs fresh parsley

6 peppercorns

½ lemon, sliced

1½ packets (¼ ounce each) gelatin

2-inch piece cucumber, thinly sliced

6 sprigs fresh dill to serve

Serves 6

This is a quick and easy version of the classic whole poached salmon. By using salmon cutlets, the dish is ready in half the time but still looks impressive (see above) and, of course, tastes just as fabulous.

1 Place the salmon cutlets in a skillet that has a lid and add the wine, onion, celery, parsley, peppercorns and lemon. Bring to a boil, reduce the heat and simmer covered for 10 minutes. Remove the pan from the heat and leave to cool—the salmon continues to cook gently as the liquid cools.

2 Dissolve the gelatin according to the packet instructions and leave to cool until thickened. Remove the skin from the salmon and gently pull out the center bone using your fingers. Brush a layer of gelatin over the salmon and arrange the cucumber and dill decoratively on top. Brush again with gelatin and chill in the refrigerator for 30 minutes before serving.

3 Serve the salmon with the herb dressing (see below), fresh shelled peas, beans and Seared New Potatoes (see page 65).

HERB DRESSING

Beat together ⅔ cup mayonnaise with ¼ cup chopped fresh dill in a mixing bowl. Season to taste with salt and freshly ground black pepper. Cover and chill in the refrigerator for up to 4 hours. Use as required.

ROAST MONKFISH WITH GREEN LENTILS

Lentils are an ancient source of nourishment and have been cultivated, it is believed, for 8,000 years, since neolithic times. Here, this healthy and non-fattening legume makes the perfect partner for the meaty flesh and mild, slightly sweet flavor of monkfish.

1 Preheat the oven to 375°F, 190°C, gas mark 5. Heat the oil in a saucepan and add the onions. Cook over medium heat for 5 minutes until they begin to soften. Add the green lentils and stir well.

2 Cut 4 slices crosswise from one of the lemons and set aside. Squeeze the juice from the remaining lemons. Add the juice to the pan with the lentils, stir in the chopped parsley and season with salt and black pepper. Continue to cook for 5 minutes until all the ingredients are heated through.

3 Meanwhile, cut the reserved lemon slices in half and tie 2 half-slices and a sprig of rosemary on to each piece of fish with string. Wrap the pieces of monkfish in foil and bake in the preheated oven for 8–10 minutes until the fish is opaque and the flesh begins to flake.

4 Remove the fish from the oven, carefully remove the string, lemon and rosemary and serve on a bed of warm green lentils.

FOR THE LENTILS

1½ tablespoons sunflower oil

2 red onions, peeled and cut into eight wedges

2 cans green lentils, each weighing 15 ounces, rinsed and drained

2 lemons

4 tablespoons chopped fresh parsley

Salt and black pepper to taste

FOR THE FISH

4 boned monkfish tails, each weighing 6 ounces

4 sprigs fresh rosemary

Serves 4

STRIPED MULLET WITH GOOSEBERRIES

The tartness of gooseberries brings a lively tang to this recipe which goes well with the fish. If possible, try to buy the mullet with the liver still intact as this has a wonderful flavor.

1 Clean the mullet thoroughly (leaving the liver intact, if possible). Trim the fins and tail and make two or three slashes in the sides of each fish with a sharp knife. Spoon a little ginger into each cavity and season the fish with salt and black pepper.

2 Heat the olive oil in a large skillet and add the striped mullet. Cook over high heat for 2 minutes on each side. Add the gooseberries and cook for 5–10 minutes until they begin to pop.

3 Add the sugar and wine to the pan and cook for a further 5 minutes, stirring frequently until the fish is cooked through and the sauce has thickened slightly. Season with salt and black pepper to taste and serve with boiled new potatoes and steamed green vegetables.

4 striped mullet or tilapia, each weighing 1 pound

1¼-inch piece ginger root peeled and chopped

Salt and black pepper to taste

1½ tablespoons olive oil

¾ pound (about 3½ cups) gooseberries, topped and tailed

3 tablespoons superfine sugar

⅔ cup white wine

Serves 4

PAELLA

Chicken, vegetables, herbs and a variety of seafood are cooked with saffron rice in this popular Spanish dish (see inset, right). Here, the chicken is boiled and the water is used for the stock—even though this takes time, it is an important step which gives the dish more flavor. Substitute the chicken with a 1 pound ham steak for an alternative.

FOR THE CHICKEN

4 boneless, skinless chicken breast halves (about 1½ pounds)

1 onion, peeled and quartered

2 bay leaves

6 peppercorns

1 teaspoon saffron strands

Bunch of fresh parsley

FOR THE RICE

3 tablespoons olive oil

1 onion, peeled and chopped

3 cloves garlic, peeled and crushed

1¾ cups Arborio risotto rice

1 pound fresh mussels, cleaned

¼ pound jumbo shrimp, cooked

3 tablespoons chopped fresh parsley

½ pound fresh shelled or frozen peas

Salt and black pepper to taste

Serves 6

1 Place the chicken breasts in a shallow pan with the onion, bay leaves, peppercorns, saffron and parsley. Cover with cold water and bring slowly to a boil. Reduce the heat and simmer for 30 minutes. Leave to cool for 10 minutes. Strain and discard all but the liquid and the chicken.

2 When cool enough, dice the chicken and set aside. Add sufficient cold water to the reserved liquid (stock) to bring the quantity up to 3⅔ cups.

3 To prepare the rice, heat the oil in a medium-sized paella pan or large shallow frying pan and add the onion and garlic. Fry over medium heat until softened, not browned. Add the rice and stir until the grains are well coated in the oil.

4 Pour in 1 ladleful of chicken stock and wait for the liquid to be fully absorbed before adding the next ladleful. Continue in this way, stirring occasionally, until the rice has absorbed half the original quantity of stock.

5 Finally, add the remaining chicken stock with the diced chicken, mussels, cooked shrimp, parsley and peas. Season with salt and black pepper and mix well so all the ingredients are combined. Simmer for 15–20 minutes, stirring occasionally, until all the chicken stock has been absorbed by the rice and the vegetables are thoroughly cooked and the mussel shells have opened. Serve immediately, directly from the pan.

FENNEL-STUFFED SEA BASS

Sea bass is infused with the flavors of fennel, scallions and thyme when the whole ensemble is baked together in a paper pocket.

6 sea bass, each weighing 1 pound

Salt and black pepper to taste

2 small bulbs fennel, trimmed and sliced

4 scallions, trimmed and sliced

3 tablespoons olive oil

6 sprigs fresh thyme

Serves 6

1 Preheat the oven to 400°F, 200°C, gas mark 6. Cut 6 sheets of wax paper into large heart-shapes at least double the size of each fish. Cut the fish into 12 fillets and season with salt and freshly ground black pepper.

2 Lay 1 fillet, skin-side down, on each sheet of wax paper, centering it on one half of the heart. Scatter each fillet with fennel and scallions and drizzle with olive oil. Place a sprig of thyme on top of the fillet and cover with another fillet, skin-side up. Bring the opposite side of the heart over to enclose the fish and fold or twist the edges over to seal. Bake in the preheated oven for 15 minutes until the flesh is opaque and flakes easily.

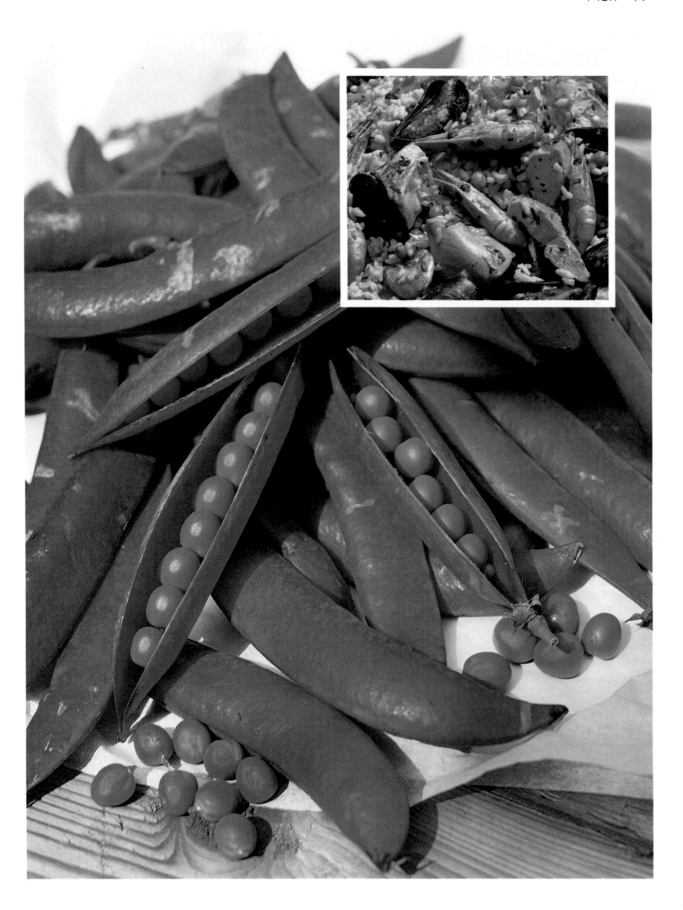

TURKEY WITH PRESERVED LEMONS & COUSCOUS

2 pounds boneless, skinless turkey breast

Salt and black pepper to taste

Grated rind and juice of 1 lemon

2 cloves garlic, peeled and chopped

4 tablespoons olive oil

6 shallots, peeled and quartered

6 ounces cremini mushrooms, halved

2 medium-sized zucchini, sliced

⅔ cup each of white wine and
chicken stock (see page 77)

6 sun-dried tomatoes, sliced

8 preserved lemon wedges (see opposite)

This exotic dish of turkey cooked with lemon, garlic, white wine and vegetables is served on a bed of parsley-flavored couscous (see below).

1 Place the turkey in a shallow dish. Stir in the salt and black pepper, lemon rind and juice and garlic. Cover and leave to marinate for 30 minutes.

2 Heat the oil in a large flameproof Dutch oven and add the shallots. Cook over medium heat until the shallots begin to brown, then add the mushrooms and zucchini and continue to cook for a further 5 minutes. Remove the vegetables using a slotted spoon and set aside.

3 Add the turkey to the Dutch oven and cook for roughly 15 minutes until brown on all sides. Return the shallots, mushrooms and zucchini to the Dutch oven, pour in the wine and stock and bring to a boil.

4 Once the liquid is boiling, stir in the tomatoes, then reduce the heat and cook for 10 minutes. Add the lemon and cook for a further 15 minutes, until the turkey is cooked through. Season with salt and black pepper.

5 To prepare the couscous, bring the stock to a boil in a saucepan that has a lid. Add the couscous, stir, then remove from the heat. Cover and leave to stand for 15 minutes until the couscous has absorbed the stock. Separate the grains with a fork, stir in the parsley and season with salt and black pepper. Divide the couscous between 4 plates and top with some turkey.

FOR THE COUSCOUS

1½ cups chicken stock (see page 77)

1½ cups couscous

4 tablespoons chopped fresh parsley

Salt and black pepper to taste

Serves 4

PRESERVING LEMONS

Wash 1 pound unwaxed lemons. Mark them into quarters and using a knife, cut almost to the center of each lemon, leaving them intact. Ease the cuts apart and spread 1 teaspoon salt inside each cut. Pack the lemons in a hot, sterilized, wide-mouth quart jar and place a disc of parchment paper (cut to size) on top. Weight down using jars and leave for 4 days in a warm room. Remove the weights and parchment, pour over lemon juice to cover the lemons, then pour over 3 tablespoons olive oil to form a thin layer. Seal and leave for 1 month.

COQ AU VIN

Chicken, bacon, onions and red wine make up this popular French dish which is traditionally thickened with softened butter and flour (beurre manié), so beware of this dish when eating out. However, rather than abstaining altogether, try this irresistible lactose-free version.

1 Immerse the onions in boiling water for 1 minute, then plunge them into cold water—the skins should now peel off easily and without any tears.

2 To prepare the chicken, heat the oil in a large Dutch oven. Add the onions and cook over medium heat for 5 minutes until golden. Stir in the bacon, garlic and mushrooms and cook for a further 10 minutes, stirring frequently. Remove the vegetables and bacon from the Dutch oven using a slotted spoon and set aside.

3 Place the chicken pieces in batches in the Dutch oven. Cook them over medium heat on all sides for 15 minutes until the skin turns golden.

4 Stir the cornstarch into the Dutch oven. Cook over low heat until the chicken begins to brown. Return the vegetables and bacon to the Dutch oven, then pour in the wine and mix well to ensure the cornstarch is blended with the wine thoroughly.

5 To prepare the bouquet garni, place the herbs and peppercorns in a square of muslin. Draw the edges of the fabric up around the herbs to form a sack and tie with string, leaving a length of string to tie around the handle of the Dutch oven for easy removal. Add the bouquet garni to the Dutch oven and bring the liquid to a boil, then simmer for 30–40 minutes. Season with salt and black pepper and garnish with chopped parsley to serve. This dish is delicious served with potatoes mashed with olive oil.

FOR THE CHICKEN

12 small white onions

4 tablespoons sunflower oil

½ pound bacon, chopped

3 cloves garlic, peeled and crushed

½ pound button mushrooms, cleaned and halved

6 boneless chicken thighs, 5 ounces each

3 boneless chicken breast halves, 7 ounces each

1½ tablespoons cornstarch

1 bottle red wine

Salt and black pepper to taste

4 tablespoons chopped fresh parsley

FOR THE BOUQUET GARNI

1 sprig each fresh parsley, thyme and sage

1 bay leaf

4 peppercorns

Serves 6

THAI GREEN CURRY

4 green chilies, halved and seeded

I stalk lemon grass, sliced

3 shallots, peeled and halved

3 cloves garlic, peeled and halved

I-inch piece galangal (Thai ginger), peeled and chopped

Grated rind of ½ lime

I teaspoon each coriander and cumin seeds

I teaspoon shrimp paste

1¾ cups canned dairy-free coconut milk

6 boneless, skinless chicken breasts or 3 boneless, skinless turkey breasts (weighing 2–2¼ pounds)

3 tablespoons Thai fish sauce (nam pla)

I tablespoon light brown sugar

I red chili, seeded and thinly sliced, grated rind of I lime and chopped fresh sweet basil or cilantro to garnish

Serves 6

Lean white meat is cooked in coconut milk and green curry paste, which gives it a distinctive flavor that is both sweet and spicy at the same time. Chicken or turkey breasts are ideal for this dish, which should be served hot with plenty of boiled rice and garnished with fresh herbs and red chili.

1 To make the curry paste, place the green chilies, lemon grass, shallots, garlic, galangal, lime rind, coriander and cumin seeds and shrimp paste in a food processor and blend to form a thick green paste. With the motor still running, gradually add half of the coconut milk and then process until all the ingredients are well combined. (Alternatively, pound the ingredients in a mortar with a pestle until a thick paste is formed, then add the milk.)

2 Place the remaining coconut milk in a large skillet and bring to a boil, then simmer for 5 minutes until reduced to half the original quantity. Stir in the prepared green curry paste and simmer for a further 5 minutes.

3 Slice the chicken breasts thinly and add to the skillet containing the reduced coconut milk. Stir in the Thai fish sauce and brown sugar and simmer for 10 minutes. The mixture will take on a slightly curdled look during cooking—this is normal. Once the chicken is tender and cooked through, serve it immediately. Divide the chicken into 6 portions and place them on individual servings of plain boiled rice. Garnish each portion with strips of red chili, a sprinkling of lime rind and chopped basil or cilantro.

MONKFISH CURRY

Monkfish, which has a meaty texture and mild flavor, makes an excellent alternative to chicken or turkey breasts in Thai Green Curry, above. Cut 2–2¼ pounds of monkfish into cubes and cook as for the chicken.

TURKEY TIKKA

2 turkey breast fillets, halved

⅓ cup plain soy yogurt

3 tablespoons concentrated tikka paste (available from some supermarkets and specialty food stores)

I lime, cut into wedges and a handful of fresh cilantro leaves to garnish

Serves 2

This simple supper dish of marinated and grilled turkey fillets can be prepared in advance and takes only minutes to cook.

1 Place the halved turkey fillets between 2 sheets of wax paper and carefully flatten them into escalopes using a rolling pin.

2 Mix together the yogurt and tikka paste and spread on to both sides of the escalopes. (Cover and chill for up to 8 hours at this point, if desired.)

3 Preheat the broiler and cook the turkey for 5–7 minutes on each side until crispy on the outside and cooked through. Garnish with lime wedges and cilantro leaves and serve on a bed of steamed rice.

PHEASANT PIE

A contemporary version of a classic English dish, this recipe combines pheasant and hearty vegetables under a "pastry" crust, proving once and for all that cooking without dairy products need not be a limitation.

1 Bone the pheasants and cut the meat into chunks. Heat the oil in a large Dutch oven and add the leek, parsnips, carrots and fennel. Cook over medium heat for 10 minutes, stirring frequently. Then remove the vegetables from the Dutch oven using a slotted spoon and set aside.

2 Add the pheasant meat to the Dutch oven and stir-fry over high heat for 10 minutes, until browned. Sprinkle the flour over the meat and add the grated rind and juice of the oranges and the stock. Mix well to combine all the ingredients. Return the vegetables to the Dutch oven with the parsley and season with salt and black pepper. Slowly bring to a boil, reduce the heat and simmer for 20 minutes.

3 Meanwhile, preheat the oven to 400°F, 200°C, gas mark 6 and prepare the pastry (see below). Then place 4 individual deep dish pans (4-inches deep) on a baking sheet and divide the pheasant mixture between the pans.

4 Divide the pastry into 4 and roll out each piece on a lightly floured work surface until large enough to cover each pie. Use the pastry trimmings to make a rim on the top lip of each dish, then dampen the pastry rim with cold water and cover with a pastry lid. Pinch the edges together to seal. Brush the tops of the pies with beaten egg yolk to glaze. Make a small hole in the pastry to allow steam to escape. Bake in the oven for 20 minutes until the pastry is golden brown. Serve immediately with Caramelized Apple Rings (see below) and shredded and steamed Savoy cabbage.

2 pheasants

3 tablespoons olive oil

1 leek, trimmed and sliced

½ pound parsnips, peeled and sliced

½ pound carrots, peeled and sliced

1 bulb fennel, trimmed and sliced

3 tablespoons all-purpose flour

Grated rind and juice of 2 oranges

1⅓ cups chicken stock (see page 77)

4 tablespoons chopped fresh parsley

Salt and black pepper to taste

1 recipe pie pastry (see below)

1 egg yolk to glaze

Serves 4

CARAMELIZED APPLE RINGS
Core 4 apples and slice into thin rings. Heat ⅓ cup of olive oil in a frying pan and stir in 3 tablespoons of confectioners' sugar. Add the apple rings and cook over high heat for 4–5 minutes until the apples brown and soften. Warm 4 tablespoons of Calvados in a separate saucepan and ignite it with a lit taper. Pour the flaming alcohol over the apples and stir until the flames die down.

PIE PASTRY
Sieve 2½ cups of all-purpose flour into a bowl. Add a pinch of salt and ¾ cup and 2 tablespoons of vegetable shortening. Rub in the shortening with your fingertips until it resembles fine breadcrumbs. Add 1 egg yolk and continue to mix. Then stir in sufficient iced water, 1 tablespoon at a time, until a soft but not sticky dough is formed. (Alternatively, place all the ingredients into a food processor and blend.) Turn out the pastry on to a floured work surface and knead. Shape the dough into a ball, wrap it in plastic wrap and chill in the refrigerator for 30 minutes before use. (Makes 1 pound.)

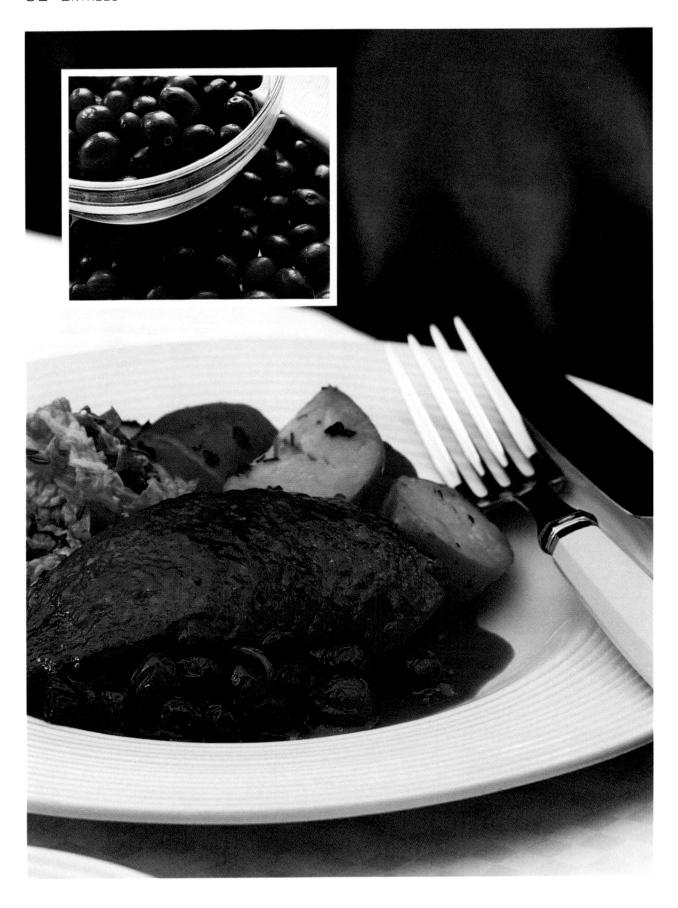

CORNISH GAME HENS WITH STICKY GLAZE

Little, single-serving chickens, Cornish game hens are not at all gamey, they are lean and tasty and—with this sauce based on orange liqueur—utterly delicious.

1 Preheat the oven to 425°F, 220°C, gas mark 7. Place the Cornish game hens into a roasting pan. Mix together the oil, honey, juniper berries and the rind and juice of the clementine in a bowl. Season with salt and black pepper. Stir the mixture until well combined, then spoon it over the hens. Roast them in the preheated oven for 40 minutes, basting occasionally.

2 Place the cooked Cornish game hens on to a serving platter and cover with foil to keep warm. To prepare the sauce, place the chopped onion into the roasting pan the game hens were cooked in and cook on the stovetop over high heat until they begin to brown. Add the Cointreau to the pan and boil until the mixture reduces by half.

3 Remove the inner pith from the clementine rind, then cut it into thin strips. Heat the oil in a skillet and cook the strips until crispy. When ready to serve, spoon this glaze over the hens. Serve with the sauce, Fennel and Snow Pea Stir-fry (see page 72) and Seared New Potatoes (see page 65).

FOR THE CORNISH GAME HENS

4 Cornish game hens

3 tablespoons olive oil

3 tablespoons honey

2 teaspoons juniper berries, crushed

Thinly sliced rind and juice of 1 clementine

Salt and black pepper to taste

FOR THE SAUCE

1 onion, peeled and finely chopped

5 teaspoons Cointreau

Rind of 1 clementine

1 tablespoon olive oil

Serves 4

DUCK WITH CRANBERRIES

Tart red cranberries go very well with succulent and sweet marmalade-coated duck breasts (see left).

1 Pierce the duck skin in several places gently with a fork. Place the duck breasts, skin-side down, in a large skillet and cook over low heat until the fat trapped between the skin and the flesh begins to run (this process is called searing and it stops the meat from drying out during cooking). Increase the heat to a medium setting and cook for 5 minutes on each side until the skin is crisp and golden. Drain all but roughly 3 tablespoons of the fat and add the shallot to the pan. Cook for 3 minutes until transparent.

2 Brush the duck breasts with the marmalade, then cook them over very high heat until the marmalade coating caramelizes.

3 Mix 1½ tablespoons of the orange juice with the arrowroot until smooth. Add it to the pan containing the duck, along with the cranberries and the grated rind and remaining juice of the orange. Mix well, reduce the heat and simmer for 10 minutes until the cranberries pop and the juice reduces by half and thickens. Stir in the thyme and season with salt and black pepper. Serve with boiled yukon gold potatoes and stir-fried green cabbage with caraway seeds, if desired.

4 boneless duck breasts, with skin (about 1½ pounds in total)

1 shallot, peeled and finely chopped

⅓ cup thick-cut marmalade

Grated rind and juice of 2 oranges

1 teaspoon arrowroot

½ pound (about 2 cups) fresh or frozen cranberries

3 tablespoons chopped fresh thyme

Salt and black pepper to taste

Serves 4

VENISON & VEGETABLE POT PIES

FOR THE FILLING

3 tablespoons sunflower oil

I onion, peeled and sliced

2 sticks celery, rinsed and chopped

2 medium-sized parsnips (approximately ½ pound), peeled and chopped

I large carrot (weighing approximately ¼ pound), scrubbed and sliced

1½ tablespoons all-purpose flour

½ teaspoon dried rosemary

1½ pounds venison, diced

1⅓ cups game stock

3 tablespoons chopped fresh parsley

FOR THE PASTRY TOPPING

¼ pound filo pastry, 8 sheets measuring approximately 12 x 16-inches

I egg, beaten, to glaze

Serves 4

These individual venison and winter vegetable pot pies are topped with paper-thin filo pastry and are impressive enough to serve at a dinner party. They can be made well in advance, assembled and frozen for up to one month. When it comes to entertaining, all you need to do is thaw the pies in the refrigerator for twelve hours, then place them in a preheated oven as your guests arrive.

1 Preheat the oven to 400°F, 200°C, gas mark 6. To prepare the filling, heat the oil in a large saucepan and add the onion and the celery. Cook over medium heat for 3–4 minutes until softened but not browned. Stir in the parsnips and carrots and cook for a further 5 minutes. Remove the vegetables from the pan using a slotted spoon and set aside.

2 Place the flour and rosemary in a large plastic freezer bag. Add the diced venison to the bag, then seal and shake it vigorously until the meat is evenly coated with the seasoned flour. Place the venison in the saucepan that was used to cook the vegetables and cook in the hot oil over high heat until brown on all sides.

3 Return the vegetables to the pan with the game stock and the chopped parsley. Stir well, reduce the heat and simmer covered for 40 minutes, stirring frequently. Remove the pan from the heat and divide the venison mixture between 4 ovenproof 10-ounce ramekins.

4 To prepare the pastry, cut the filo sheets into squares that are large enough to easily fit over the top of each pie. To prevent the filo pastry from drying out, keep it covered with a clean, damp tea towel until ready to use. Brush the rim of each ramekin with beaten egg and layer 4 filo pastry sheets on top of each pie, pressing them down on to the rims of the ramekins to seal the ingredients. Place the ramekins on a baking tray and bake in the preheated oven for 10 minutes until the pastry is golden. Serve immediately with green vegetables.

LAMB OR PORK POT PIES
Substitute the venison with 1½ pounds of either diced lamb or pork and follow the recipe above, using lamb stock (see page 77) or pork stock as appropriate.

BEEF SALAD

The strong flavors of spicy red chilies, sweet cherry tomatoes, woody shiitake mushrooms and toasted sesame seeds combine to create a wonderfully hot and tasty beef salad (see above).

1 Cook the beef under a preheated broiler for 1–4 minutes, depending on how well you like your meat cooked. Leave to cool, then slice very thinly.

2 Seed and slice the chilies, then slice the mushrooms, discarding the woody stems. Heat the oil in a frying pan, add the chilies and mushrooms and stir-fry over high heat for 5 minutes, stirring occasionally.

3 Place the sesame seeds in a heavy-based skillet and cook over low heat for 1–2 minutes, stirring occasionally until the seeds are toasted. Arrange the lettuce leaves, endive, tomatoes and cucumber on 4 serving plates. Place the beef slices and mushroom mixture over the salad and scatter the sesame seeds over each portion. Serve with crusty bread rolls.

1 pound top sirloin or rib steak

1 red and 1 yellow chili

¼ pound shiitake mushrooms

3 tablespoons olive oil

3 tablespoons sesame seeds

1 green leaf lettuce, washed and sliced

1 head Belgian endive, leaves separated

2 cups cherry tomatoes, halved

1¼-inch piece of cucumber, thinly sliced

Serves 4

LAMB TIKKA

Tikka is the Indian equivalent of the Turkish kebab, in that pieces of meat (usually chicken or lamb) are marinated in a spicy tikka paste, threaded on to skewers and then grilled. As the paste cooks, it creates a tasty coating for the tender meat.

1 Cut the lamb into 2-inch cubes and place in a shallow dish. Blend the oil, tikka paste, garlic and coconut milk in a bowl. Pour the mixture over the lamb and toss to coat the meat evenly. Cover and leave to marinate at room temperature for 30 minutes or chill in the refrigerator for up to 12 hours.

2 Soak 8 wooden skewers in water to prevent them scorching. Remove the lamb from the marinade and divide into 8 piles. Thread each pile on to a skewer. Cook the kebabs under a preheated broiler for 3–8 minutes on each side until the meat is brown on the outside and cooked through.

3 Cook the rice according to the packet instructions, adding the turmeric to the cooking water. Garnish the kebabs with coriander and serve with the turmeric rice, mini naans and fruit chutney.

2 pounds lean lamb

3 tablespoons olive oil

3 tablespoons concentrated tikka paste (available from some supermarkets and specialty food stores)

2 cloves garlic, peeled, coarsely chopped

⅔ cup dairy-free coconut milk

1⅔ cup basmati rice

½ teaspoon powdered turmeric

Chopped fresh cilantro to garnish

4 mini naan breads or regular naan (halved) and fruit chutney to serve

Serves 4

ROAST LAMB WITH SHIITAKE STUFFING

The Japanese have made use of the meaty flesh and full-bodied, woody flavor of shiitake mushrooms for over 2,000 years. Here, they give the traditional dish of roasted rack of lamb (see left) additional flavor with an exotic hint of the East.

1 Preheat the oven to 425°F, 220°C, gas mark 7. To prepare the stuffing, heat the oil in a skillet and add the scallions and garlic. Cook over medium heat for 5 minutes until softened, not browned. Add the mushrooms and ginger and cook for a further 5 minutes, stirring frequently. Remove the pan from the heat and leave the mixture to cool. Once cool, stir well, then beat in the egg yolk and rosemary and season with salt and black pepper.

2 To prepare the lamb, season it with salt and black pepper and spread with the cranberry sauce. Spoon the stuffing into the center of a roasting pan and set the two racks of lamb on top, bone-side down.

3 Place the lamb in the preheated oven and roast for either 30 minutes for rare lamb, or for 45 minutes if you like your lamb fairly well done. When ready to serve, remove the lamb from the oven and cut between the ribs to separate the meat into chops. Divide the stuffing into 4 portions, place on serving plates and arrange the lamb chops attractively around the stuffing. Serve with a side dish of mixed baby vegetables and grilled polenta.

1 tablespoon olive oil

4 scallions, trimmed, quartered and cut into 1-inch lengths

2 cloves garlic, peeled and crushed

¼ pound shiitake mushrooms, the bases trimmed

1-inch fresh ginger, peeled and chopped

1 egg yolk

1 tablespoon chopped fresh rosemary

Salt and black pepper to taste

2 center-cut racks of lamb, trimmed

1 tablespoon cranberry sauce

Serves 4

Lamb & Apricot Cobbler

*Dried apricots add sweetness to this exotic and warming
lamb, mushroom and cranberry dish. It is topped with a tasty seasoned
scone crust which finishes the dish off neatly and makes
it a more substantial meal.*

FOR THE LAMB

3 tablespoons olive oil

I onion, peeled and coarsely chopped

½ pound cremini mushrooms, sliced

1½ tablespoons all-purpose flour

I teaspoon mixed spice (or a pinch each
of ground cinnamon, ground cloves and
ground ginger)

1¾ pounds lean lamb, cubed

1¼ cups lamb stock (see page 77)

6 ounces (about 1¾ cups) dried apricots

6 ounces (about 1½ cups) fresh or frozen
cranberries

Salt and black pepper to taste

FOR THE SCONE TOPPING

1¼ cups self-rising flour

I teaspoon baking powder

3 tablespoons vegetable shortening

I large egg

3 tablespoons chopped fresh parsley

Serves 4

1 To prepare the lamb, heat the oil in a large Dutch oven and add the onion and mushrooms. Cook over low heat until softened.

2 Place the flour and mixed spice into a large freezer bag and add the cubed lamb. Seal the bag and shake it vigorously to coat the meat evenly in the seasoned flour mixture.

3 Add the seasoned lamb to the pan with onions and mushrooms and stir. Increase the heat to a high setting and cook for 5–10 minutes until the lamb is evenly browned.

4 Add the stock to the pan and slowly bring to a boil. Reduce the heat and simmer for 15 minutes, stirring occasionally. Finally, stir in the apricots and cranberries and simmer for a further 5 minutes. Remove from the heat and set aside.

5 Preheat the oven to 400°F, 200°C, gas mark 6. To prepare the scone topping, sift the flour and baking powder into a mixing bowl. Rub in the fat with your fingertips until the mixture resembles fine breadcrumbs. Beat together the egg, 6 tablespoons cold water and the parsley in a separate bowl, then add to the flour mixture. Mix until a soft, not sticky, dough is formed. Roll out the dough on a lightly floured work surface until roughly ¾-inch-thick and cut out several 2-inch circles.

6 Arrange the scone shapes around the edge of the hot lamb. Then bake in the preheated oven for 25 minutes until the scones are puffed and golden brown. Serve the Lamb & Apricot Cobbler with green beans.

WHOLEWHEAT SCONE TOPPING
Substitute the self-rising flour with 1¼ cups wholewheat flour. Sift it with 2¼ teaspoons baking powder and rub in the fat with your fingertips as step 5, above. Beat the egg with 6 tablespoons of cold water and 3 tablespoons of toasted sunflower seeds (in place of the parsley). The wholewheat topping makes this dish more substantial, for those extra chilly winter evenings!

FRUITY RABBIT STEW
Substitute the pork in Fruity Pork Stew (see below) with 2 jointed rabbits. Cut the meat into cubes and place in a freezer bag with the flour and 1 teaspoon dry mustard (in place of mixed spice). Substitute the apricots with an equal quantity of prunes and cook as below. Serve with couscous. Rabbit has a mild flavor which is delicious with the spiced fruits.

FRUITY PORK STEW

During the cold winter months, one of the easiest ways of entertaining is with a hearty pork stew that can bubble away happily on the stove until you are ready to eat. In this recipe, cubes of lean pork are cooked slowly with dried apricots, spices and plenty of red wine until the meat is very tender and succulent (see above).

1 Place the flour and mixed spice into a large freezer bag and add the cubed pork. Seal the bag and shake it vigorously to coat the meat evenly in the seasoned flour mixture. Heat half the oil in a large Dutch oven over medium heat. Cook the meat in batches for roughly 10 minutes, until the meat is evenly browned. Remove the last batch from the Dutch oven using a slotted spoon and set aside with the rest of the browned meat.

2 Heat the remaining oil in the Dutch oven. Add the onion and celery and cook over high heat for 5 minutes, until the onions are softened, but not browned. Add the mushrooms and continue to cook for a further 3–4 minutes, stirring continuously.

3 Return the browned pork to the Dutch oven with the apricots, raisins, apples and grated rind and juice of the orange and mix thoroughly. Add the red wine and parsley and season with salt and black pepper.

4 Bring the liquid in the Dutch oven to a boil, then simmer uncovered for 2–2½ hours, stirring occasionally, until the meat is tender and the liquid is thickened. Serve Fruity Pork Stew with couscous (see page 49).

¼ cup all-purpose flour

1 teaspoon mixed spice (see opposite)

2 pounds boneless pork loin, cubed

4 tablespoons sunflower oil

1 large onion, peeled and finely chopped

2 sticks celery

¼ pound cremini mushrooms, sliced

¼ pound ready-to-eat apricots, halved

⅓ cup raisins

2 apples, peeled, cored and chopped

Grated rind and juice of 1 orange

1 bottle red wine

4 tablespoons chopped fresh flat-leaf parsley

Salt and black pepper to taste

Serves 6

VEGETABLE STIR-FRY

This is a delicious and healthy vegetarian main course, which is packed with fresh, crunchy vegetables and cooked very rapidly in hot oil. This Oriental style of cooking food is one of the fastest and most nutritious methods of cooking. You do not necessarily need a wok; I find a good quality large skillet heated with oil until it is almost at smoking point cooks any stir-fry dish to perfection.

1   Heat the oil in a large skillet or wok and add the onion and garlic. Cook over high heat for 5 minutes until softened.

2   Add the peppers, baby corn, zucchini, snow peas and mushrooms and stir-fry for 5 minutes until the vegetables are just softened and begin to turn brown. Stir the mixture frequently to prevent the vegetables sticking to the base of the pan and burning.

3   Meanwhile, stir-fry or boil the noodles in a separate saucepan, according to the packet instructions. Once cooked, stir the plum sauce into the noodles and serve with the stir-fried vegetables.

3 tablespoons canola or olive oil

1 large onion, peeled and sliced

2 cloves garlic, peeled and finely chopped

1 red bell pepper, seeded and sliced

1 green bell pepper, seeded and sliced

1 orange bell pepper, seeded and sliced

4 ounces baby corn, trimmed and halved

1 medium zucchini, cut into thick strips

4 ounces snow peas, halved

6 ounces enoki mushrooms, trimmed

8 ounces dried Oriental noodles

⅓ cup plum sauce

Serves 4 (or 6–8 as a side dish)

CHICKEN AND SUMMER VEGETABLE STIR-FRY

Slice 4 boneless and skinless chicken breast halves (about 1½ pounds) into fine strips. Heat 3 tablespoons of olive oil in a large skillet or wok and add the chicken strips. Stir-fry over high heat for 5 minutes, until the chicken turns golden brown.

Add 4 sliced scallions, 2 crushed garlic cloves, 1 green and 1 yellow bell pepper, seeded and sliced, ¾ pound of baby carrots, halved lengthwise and ½ pound of trimmed string beans to the pan. Stir-fry for 8 minutes. Finally, add 3 tablespoons of soy sauce and season with black pepper. Serve this stir-fry with plain boiled rice or noodles.

DUCK AND SUMMER VEGETABLE STIR-FRY

Slice 4 boneless and skinless duck breast halves into fine strips. Heat 3 tablespoons of olive oil in a large skillet and add the strips of duck. Cook over high heat for 4–5 minutes until the duck is brown on the outside but remains slightly pink in the middle. Then add the prepared vegetables as for Chicken and Summer Vegetable Stir-fry and cook as instructed above.

STIR-FRY TIPS

A stir-fry is, essentially, cooked rapidly, so it is vital when making it to prepare all the ingredients in advance, so that they are ready to throw into the pan when required. Vegetables and meat should be cut into strips.

For best results, and to ensure that the meat and vegetables are cooked quickly, the oil should be almost smoking before any of the ingredients are added to the pan.

It is advisable to stir the mixture constantly during cooking to ensure that each part of the stir-fry is evenly cooked and does not burn or stick.

Vegetable &
Side Dishes

CURRIED SWEET POTATO

The pleasing sweetness of this brightly colored vegetable marries surprisingly well with the flavors of crushed red pepper and garam masala (a combination of roasted spices), to produce a sweet and spicy side dish (see above).

1½ pounds sweet potatoes, peeled and cubed

⅓ cup olive oil

1 teaspoon red pepper flakes

1 tablespoon garam masala

⅔ cup vegetable stock (see page 77)

Serves 6

1 Place the cubed potatoes in a large saucepan, cover with cold water and bring to a boil. Reduce the heat and simmer for 5 minutes. Then drain and set aside.

2 Heat the oil in a large skillet that has a lid and add the crushed red pepper flakes and garam masala. Cook over medium heat for 2 minutes, stirring constantly until the spices are well blended with the oil.

3 Add the potatoes to the pan and stir well so the spices and oil coat each piece of potato. Then add the vegetable stock and bring the liquid to a boil, stirring constantly.

4 Reduce the heat and simmer covered for 15 minutes, stirring occasionally until the potatoes are tender. Remove the potatoes from the pan and place them on a warmed serving dish. Serve with chicken, shrimp or lamb curry.

SEARED NEW POTATOES WITH ROSEMARY & SEA SALT

New potatoes are perfect for frying. To give them additional flavor and a wonderful fragrance, cook them in olive oil with a few sprigs of rosemary. When buying new potatoes, ensure the skin rubs away easily and select the smallest ones in order to speed up the cooking time.

⅓ cup extra virgin olive oil

2 pounds new or small potatoes, washed

I teaspoon sea salt

Black pepper to taste

6 sprigs fresh rosemary

Serves 4–6

1   Pour the olive oil into a large heavy-based saucepan that has a lid and cook over high heat until sizzling. Add the potatoes and salt to the hot oil—do this carefully because the oil is likely to spit as you add the salt. Cover the pan with a lid and cook the potatoes for 10 minutes, shaking the pan frequently to prevent them scorching.

2   Add the black pepper and rosemary and stir well to coat the potatoes. Cover the pan again and cook for a further 5–10 minutes. Stir the potatoes several times during cooking to ensure they do not burn. Remove them from the pan and place them in a warmed serving bowl. This dish is delicious served with Poached Salmon (see page 44), Herb-coated Turkey (see page 28) and Cornish Game Hens with Sticky Glaze (see page 53).

POTATO CAKES

Potato Cakes are quick and easy to prepare and are highly versatile— use them as an alternative to a side dish of boiled potatoes or, for a special treat, serve them for breakfast with poached eggs.

1½ pounds potatoes, peeled

3 scallions, washed and trimmed

I large egg

2 teaspoons wholegrain mustard

Salt and black pepper to taste

3 tablespoons olive oil

Serves 4

1   Grate the potatoes on to a sheet of paper towel and pat dry. Then place into a large mixing bowl.

2   Finely slice the scallions and stir them into the grated potato. Stir in the egg and mustard. Season with salt and black pepper.

3   Heat the oil in a large skillet over high heat. Take a tablespoon of the potato mixture and, using a second spoon, push the mixture off the first spoon into the hot oil. Repeat until the frying pan is full. Cook the potato cakes for 4–5 minutes on each side until browned and cooked through. Remove from the pan and place on paper towel to absorb any excess oil. Keep this first batch warm while frying the second batch in the same way.

PERFECT BAKED POTATOES

4 baking potatoes (each weighing approximately 6 ounces)

Coarse sea salt to taste

3 tablespoons light, untoasted sesame oil

Serves 4

It is surprisingly simple to cook a baked potato badly—with rubbery skin and dried-out flesh. But it is also easy to do it well. The best way to achieve perfection every time—with crispy skins and soft flesh—is to coat the potatoes in sesame oil, sprinkle them with sea salt and bake them in a hot oven for one hour. You can then stuff them using any of the fillings below (each recipe fills four potatoes) and serve them on their own or with a selection of cold meats or smoked fish.

1 Preheat the oven to 400°F, 200°C, gas mark 6. Wash the potatoes and prick them in several places with a fork. Pat them dry with paper towel.

2 Sit the potatoes in a roasting pan and sprinkle with sea salt. Drizzle the sesame oil over the potatoes and bake in the preheated oven for 1 hour, until the skins are dark and crispy. Use a fork or a knife to pierce the potatoes—if the flesh is soft, the potatoes are cooked through.

3 Remove the potatoes from the pan and place on serving plates. To fill them, cut halfway into each potato using a sharp knife and gently press the potatoes open with your fingers. Spoon your chosen filling (see below) into the opened-out potato and serve immediately.

BACON, OLIVE AND SPINACH FILLING
Chop 5 ounces of Canadian bacon into small pieces. Place in a skillet and cook over low heat until the fat begins to run. Add ⅓ cup of pitted and halved black olives, and 1½ cups of trimmed young spinach leaves to the pan and continue to cook for 2–3 minutes until the spinach just begins to wilt. Remove from the pan and carefully spoon the mixture into the potatoes to serve.

AVOCADO AND SHRIMP FILLING
Peel, stone and chop 1 large avocado and place the flesh in a bowl. Stir in the grated rind and juice of 1 lime, taking care not to mash the avocado flesh. Then add ½ pound of cooked shrimp and season with plenty of black pepper. Spoon the mixture into the potatoes to serve.

TOMATO AND SMOKED TOFU FILLING
Heat 3 tablespoons of oil in a saucepan and add 1 peeled and chopped onion and 2 peeled and crushed cloves of garlic. Cook over medium heat until soft. Stir in a 15-ounce can of chopped tomatoes and 1½ cups of cubed smoked tofu. Cook over high heat until the mixture thickens. Add 3 tablespoons of chopped fresh cilantro, season with salt and black pepper and spoon into the potatoes.

CORNED BEEF AND HORSERADISH FILLING
Scoop the potato flesh out of the potato skins using a spoon. Place the skins in the oven to keep warm. Beat the potato flesh in a bowl with 4 tablespoons of grated horseradish. Fold in 10 ounces of cubed corned beef and 3 tablespoons of snipped fresh chives. Spoon the mixture into the potato skins and serve.

Zucchini with Bell Pepper, Garlic & Rosemary

3 tablespoons olive oil

1 red bell pepper, seeded and sliced

2 pounds zucchini, trimmed and sliced

3 cloves garlic, peeled and sliced

8 sprigs fresh rosemary

Salt and black pepper to taste

Serves 4

This colorful vegetable dish is very quick to prepare and the wonderfully fragrant flavors of garlic and rosemary marry well with the sweet red pepper and zucchini.

1 Heat the oil in a large skillet and add the red bell pepper. Cook over high heat for 5 minutes until the pepper begins to soften.

2 Add the zucchini and garlic. Continue to cook over high heat for a further 6 minutes until the zucchini and peppers become tender and begin to brown.

3 Add the rosemary sprigs and season with salt and black pepper. Cook for a further 2 minutes, stirring constantly. Serve the vegetables hot with roast meats or steamed fish.

Orange-glazed Baby Carrots

1 pound baby carrots, trimmed

1 tablespoon coriander seeds, lightly crushed with a pestle in a mortar

⅓ cup orange juice

Salt to taste

Serves 4

The secret to this recipe is to cook the carrots very gently in order to retain their natural sweetness—doing so in orange juice enhances their flavor.

1 Gently remove any dirt from the carrots and rinse under running cold water. Place in a large mixing bowl.

2 Stir the coriander seeds and orange juice into the carrots and mix well. Season with salt.

3 Place the mixture in a large saucepan and cook over low heat for 8 minutes until the carrots are tender and the juice reduces to a sticky glaze. Serve with roast spring lamb.

ORANGE-GLAZED SWEET POTATOES AND PARSNIPS
As with baby carrots, sweet potatoes and parsnips have a wonderfully sweet taste that works well with the flavor of oranges.

Peel and cube 1 medium-sized sweet potato and 2 parsnips and place them in a large mixing bowl. Stir in ⅓ cup of orange juice and 1 tablespoon of lightly bruised fenugreek seeds in place of the coriander seeds and mix well until the vegetables are well coated. Season with salt to taste and place the mixture in a large saucepan. Cook for 12–15 minutes until the vegetables are soft. Serve with roast beef.

PUMPKIN WITH CARAWAY SEEDS

In this recipe, the addition of caraway seeds adds a nutty, aromatic taste to the mild and sweet flavor of roasted pumpkins. The pumpkin flesh is shaped with a melon baller, but if you find the flesh is too firm, simply cut it into cubes using a knife. When buying pumpkins, always choose those that are free from skin blemishes and seem heavy for their size.

1 Preheat the oven to 425°F, 220°C, gas mark 7. Shape the pumpkin flesh into balls using a melon baller, or chop it into cubes using a knife.

2 Heat the fat in a small roasting pan on the stovetop until sizzling. Then, carefully add the pumpkin balls and stir well to coat them thoroughly in the fat. Roast in the preheated oven for 30 minutes until the pumpkin is just tender and lightly browned.

3 Place a heavy-based skillet over high heat for 1 minute. Reduce the heat and add the caraway seeds. Cook over low heat for 1–2 minutes, stirring occasionally until the seeds are well toasted, then set aside.

4 Drain the pumpkin balls, place them in a serving bowl with the toasted caraway seeds and stir to mix the ingredients thoroughly. Season with salt and black pepper. Serve hot with roast pork.

1¼ pounds (about 4 cups once cubed) pumpkin flesh, skinned and seeded

⅓ cup vegetable shortening

3 tablespoons caraway seeds

Salt and black pepper to taste

Serves 4

PATTYPAN RISOTTO

Patty pans are miniature squash that are either bright yellow or green in color. They are delicious steamed, fried or cooked with rice, as in this delicious vegetarian dish. The best thing about this particular risotto recipe is that it is made in the oven so there is no need to stand by the stove stirring it all the time!

1 Preheat the oven to 425°F, 220°C, gas mark 7. Place the oil, scallions and garlic into a large roasting pan and place on the floor of the oven. Cook for 5 minutes until the scallions are soft.

2 Remove the pan from the oven and add the rice. Stir well to coat all the grains thoroughly in the oil. Stir in the stock and return the pan to the floor of the oven. Cook for a further 20 minutes.

3 Remove the pan from the oven and add the black pepper and pattypans to the rice mixture. Stir to combine all the ingredients. Cover the tin with foil and return it to the floor of the oven. Cook for a further 20 minutes until the rice is tender and it has absorbed the stock completely and the patty pans are cooked. Serve sprinkled with soy cheese, if desired.

3 tablespoons olive oil

4 scallions, peeled and chopped

2 cloves garlic, peeled and crushed

1¾ cups risotto rice (see page 12)

3⅔ cups vegetable stock (see page 77)

Black pepper to taste

1 pound green and yellow pattypans, peeled, trimmed and quartered

Freshly grated soy cheese to serve (optional)

Serves 4 (or 2 as an entrée)

Mediterranean Stuffed Eggplant

Eggplant filled with a colorful mix of peppers, tomatoes, onions and herbs are a perfect light meal for non-meat eaters (see below) as well as a substantial vegetable side dish, ideal with grilled meats and fish.

4 medium-sized eggplant
(each weighing approximately ¾ pound)

3 tablespoons extra virgin olive oil

4 scallions, trimmed and sliced

2 cloves garlic, peeled and
finely chopped

2 large bell peppers, 1 yellow and
1 green, seeded and chopped

4 ripe tomatoes, quartered and seeded

3 tablespoons dried oregano

Salt and black pepper to taste

Fresh oregano leaves to garnish

Serves 8 (or 4 as a main course)

1 Preheat the oven to 400°F, 200°C, gas mark 6. Cut each of the eggplant in half lengthwise, then carefully scoop out the flesh from each eggplant using a spoon, leaving the skin (and a layer of flesh to reinforce the skin) as a case. Lightly brush the inside and outside of each case with some of the olive oil, then set the skins aside.

2 Cut the eggplant flesh into chunks. Heat the remaining oil in a large skillet and add the eggplant flesh, scallions and garlic. Cook over high heat for 3 minutes until the vegetables are soft.

3 Add the chopped peppers and the tomatoes to the pan with the eggplant and scallions and continue to cook for a further 5 minutes until the vegetables begin to brown. Stir in the dried oregano and season the mixture with salt and black pepper.

4 Arrange the eggplant cases side-by-side on a large baking sheet and fill them with the cooked vegetable mixture.

5 Bake in the preheated oven for 15 minutes, until the eggplant cases are cooked through, but still hold their shape and the vegetable fillings are piping hot. To serve, garnish with the oregano leaves.

EGGPLANT CAVIAR

Preheat the oven to 400°F, 200°C, gas mark 6. Cut 3 medium-sized eggplant (each weighing approximately ¾ pound) in half and score the flesh with a knife. Place in a roasting pan and cook in the preheated oven for 25 minutes until soft and cooked through.

Scoop the flesh out of the cooked eggplant using a metal spoon and place in a food processor. Blend with 2 cloves of garlic and ½ cup of olive oil. (Alternatively, mash the flesh in a mixing bowl with a potato masher and mix in the chopped garlic, then gradually blend in the oil.) Season with salt and black pepper to taste and serve on toast or as a dip with vegetable crudités.

GNOCCHI-TOPPED VEGETABLES

Gnocchi are small Italian dumplings made from flour, semolina and potato starch. (Do check the label if using shop-bought gnocchi since many varieties contain skimmed milk.) Gnocchi are certainly very versatile—they can be baked, steamed or fried—and combined with a whole host of savory sauces. In this recipe, I have used them as a quick and simple topping to a robust and tasty vegetable mixture.

FOR THE VEGETABLES

3 tablespoons olive oil

1 onion, peeled and chopped

2 cloves garlic, peeled and crushed

2 large bell peppers, 1 red and 1 green, seeded and chopped

2 zucchini, medium-sized, halved and sliced

15-ounce can chopped tomatoes

Salt and black pepper to taste

FOR THE TOPPING

14 ounces fresh gnocchi

3 tablespoons olive oil

Serves 4 (or 2 as a main course)

1 Preheat the oven to 400°F, 200°C, gas mark 6. To prepare the vegetables, heat the oil in a large skillet and add the onion. Cook over medium heat until softened, not browned. Add the garlic, peppers and zucchini and cook for a further 5 minutes, stirring occasionally.

2 Add the canned tomatoes and bring to a boil. Reduce the heat and simmer uncovered for 5 minutes. Season with salt and black pepper.

3 To prepare the topping, place the gnocchi in a large saucepan of boiling salted water and cook over medium heat for 2–3 minutes, or according to the packet instructions. Drain the gnocchi thoroughly.

4 Spoon the vegetable mixture into a medium-sized ovenproof dish and top with the gnocchi. Sprinkle olive oil over the gnocchi. Bake in the oven for 25 minutes until the topping is golden brown. Serve hot as an accompaniment to a lamb or pork dish or as a vegetarian main course.

FENNEL & SNOW PEA STIR-FRY

The anise-like flavor of fennel complements the subtle sweetness of snow peas in this dish that is excellent served with grilled fish.

3 tablespoons peanut oil

I bulb fennel, thinly sliced and shredded

3 scallions, trimmed and halved

¼ pound trimmed snow peas halved lengthwise

¼ pound enoki mushrooms, trimmed

⅓ cup light soy sauce

¾ cup cashew nuts, toasted and coarsely chopped

Salt and black pepper to taste

Serves 6

1 Heat the peanut oil in a wok or large frying pan and add the fennel and scallions. Stir-fry for 3 minutes, stirring constantly. Add the snow peas and mushrooms and continue to stir-fry for a further 3 minutes.

2 Keeping the pan on the heat, stir in the soy sauce and cashew nuts and season with salt and black pepper. Serve the stir-fry with grilled fish and plain boiled rice or noodles.

CELERY AND SUGAR SNAP PEA STIR-FRY
For a more subtle flavor, replace the fennel with 1 head of celery, thinly sliced. Replace the snow peas with sugar snap peas and the enoki mushrooms with ¼ pound of trimmed and halved button mushrooms.

VEGETARIAN STUFFED CABBAGE

Cabbage parcels bulging with onions and nuts are a warming dish and ideal served with fresh Tomato Sauce (see page 77). Choose a cabbage with crispy leaves that are firmly packed together.

I savoy cabbage (weighing approximately 1½ pounds)

I tablespoon olive oil

I red onion, peeled and chopped

⅓ cup pine nuts, toasted

4 tablespoons plain soy yogurt

Salt and black pepper to taste

2⅔ cups vegetable stock (see page 77)

4 sprigs fresh marjoram

6 peppercorns

Serves 4

1 Discard the outermost leaves of the cabbage. Break off the next 8 leaves and remove the core. Finely shred about ¼ cup of the remaining cabbage and reserve. Immerse the 8 whole reserved leaves in a pan of boiling water for 1 minute, rinse with cold water and leave to drain.

2 Heat the oil in a large skillet and add the onion. Cook over medium heat for 5 minutes until softened. Add the shredded cabbage and stir-fry for 2 minutes. Remove from the heat and stir in the pine nuts and yogurt. Season with salt and black pepper.

3 Lay the whole cabbage leaves on a work surface and divide the onion and pine nut filling between them. Fold the leaves over the filling to form a parcel and tie each one with string. Arrange the parcels in a single layer in a large saucepan.

4 Pour the stock over the parcels and add the marjoram and peppercorns. Bring the stock to a boil, then reduce the heat and simmer for 15 minutes. Drain the cooked cabbage parcels thoroughly, then remove the string. Place 2 parcels on each plate and serve with fresh Tomato Sauce (see page 77) or with grilled meat or fish.

RED CABBAGE WITH PEARS

For this colorful side dish (see above), red cabbage and pears are cooked gently in fruit juice to produce a deliciously sweet flavor. Serve as an accompaniment to roast meats or hearty winter stews.

1 Heat the oil over medium heat in a large heavy-based saucepan that has a lid. Add the bay leaves, juniper berries and onion. Cook for 5 minutes until the onion is softened, not browned.

2 Place the shredded red cabbage into the pan and stir until it is well coated in the oil and combined with the other ingredients. Cook over low heat for 15 minutes, stirring occasionally.

3 Add the pears, fruit juice and sugar to the pan. Stir the mixture thoroughly to combine with the other ingredients and cover. Simmer over low heat for a further 15 minutes, until the cabbage and fruit are soft. Season with salt and black pepper to serve.

1 tablespoon olive oil

2 bay leaves, lightly bruised

4 juniper berries, bruised

1 small onion, peeled and thinly sliced

1 pound red cabbage, shredded

2 pears, peeled, cored and chopped

⅔ cup pear or apple juice

¼ cup light brown sugar

Salt and black pepper to taste

Serves 4

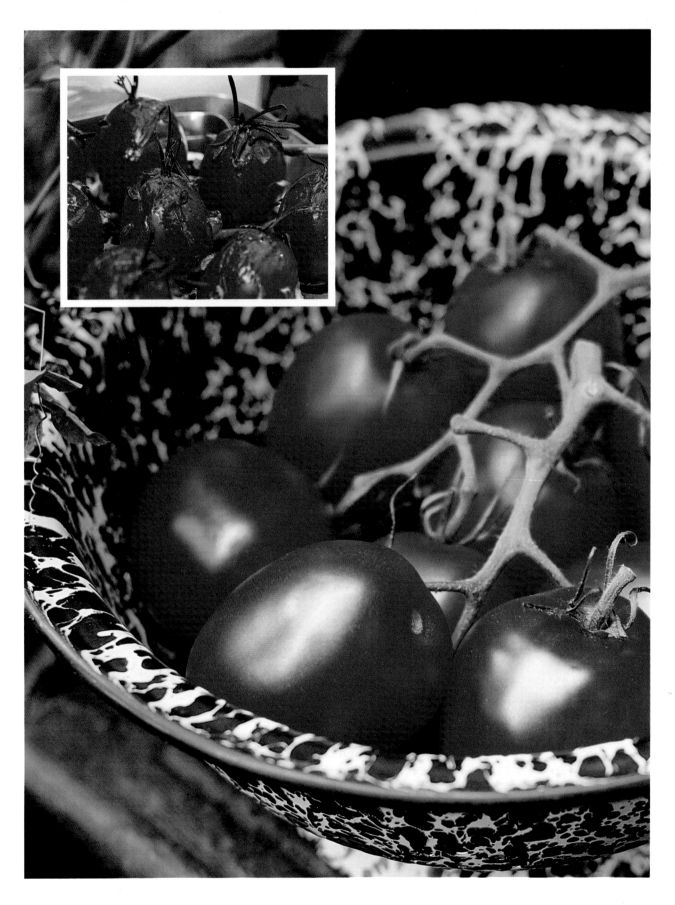

ROAST TOMATOES WITH BALSAMIC VINEGAR

Roasting plum tomatoes retains their fresh juiciness and full flavor. The exquisite taste of Italian balsamic vinegar sets off this dish with perfection. Serve the tomatoes with barbecued meats or roast poultry.

1 Preheat the oven to 425°F, 220°C, gas mark 7. Arrange the onion slices in a medium-sized ovenproof dish or baking sheet.

2 Cut a thin slice from the base of each tomato so they can sit without rolling over. Make a few small slits in the skin of each tomato and press a slice of garlic into each one. Sit the tomatoes on top of the onion slices.

3 Push a sprig of rosemary into the top of each tomato, pushing it through to pierce the onion beneath. Drizzle with oil and sprinkle with salt, pepper and sugar. Roast in the oven for 20 minutes until the tomatoes are soft and cooked through. Serve immediately, drizzled with balsamic vinegar.

1 red onion, peeled and cut into 8 slices
8 plum tomatoes
2 cloves garlic, peeled and thinly sliced
8 sprigs fresh rosemary
⅓ cup extra virgin olive oil
Coarse sea salt and cracked pepper to taste
2 teaspoons superfine sugar
Balsamic vinegar to serve
Serves 4

ROAST BABY EGGPLANT

Baby or Italian eggplant can be cooked in the same way as the tomatoes above. Use 4 baby eggplant in place of the plum tomatoes and substitute sprigs of oregano for the rosemary. Make a hole in the top of each eggplant using a skewer to allow the oregano sprigs to pierce through to the onions.

TRIPLE TOMATO & AVOCADO SALAD

I have used three types of tomato in this refreshing salad—sweet red and yellow cherry tomatoes combine perfectly with the stronger flavor of sun-dried tomato paste to create a tasty filling for creamy avocados.

1 Halve and stone the avocados. Pour the lime juice over the flesh. Fill the hollow left by the stone with the mixed cherry tomatoes.

2 Place the sun-dried tomatoes in a food processor with the oil and honey. Blend until they are well combined. (Alternatively, crush the tomatoes in a mortar with a pestle and gradually mix in the oil and honey.) Season with salt and black pepper.

3 Place a teaspoon of the tomato paste on the tomato-filled avocados, arrange the arugula leaves over the top and serve.

2 ripe avocados
1 tablespoon lime juice
2 cups each red and yellow cherry tomatoes, halved
3 sun-dried tomatoes
4 tablespoons olive oil
1 tablespoon honey
Salt and black pepper to taste
2 cups small arugula leaves
Serves 4

BASIC WHITE SAUCE

2 tablespoons non-dairy margarine

2½ tablespoons cornstarch

2 cups soy milk

Salt and black pepper to taste

Makes 2 cups

*Dairy-free white sauce is wonderfully versatile and a good substitute
for the traditional butter and milk-based version.*

1 Place the margarine in a non-stick saucepan and melt it over medium heat.
Remove the pan from the heat. Mix the cornstarch with ¼ cup of the milk
in a mixing bowl until smooth. Add to the pan and stir well.

2 Gradually add the remaining soy milk, stirring constantly to retain a
smooth texture. Return the pan to the heat and bring slowly to a boil,
stirring constantly until the sauce begins to thicken. Then, reduce the heat
and simmer for 2 minutes until thick. Season with salt and black pepper.

FLAVORINGS
A wide variety of flavorings can be added to Basic White Sauce mixture at the
end of preparation. To serve with fish, stir in 3 tablespoons of chopped fresh
mixed herbs such as dill, chervil or flat-leaf parsley. To serve with meat, stir in
3 tablespoons of chopped fresh mixed herbs such as thyme, parsley, sage or
cilantro. To serve with poultry, stir in 1 tablespoon of wholegrain mustard.

MAYONNAISE

1 large egg

Large pinch of dry mustard

Salt and black pepper to taste

1 tablespoon white wine vinegar

⅔ cup olive oil

Makes approximately ¾ cup

*This thick and "creamy" mayonnaise is easy to prepare and delicious
served with cold salads or hot fish and meat dishes.*

1 Place the egg in a food processor with the mustard, seasoning and vinegar.
Blend until all the ingredients are combined and the mixture is smooth.

2 With the motor still running, gradually add the oil, drop by drop, to form
a thick and glossy mayonnaise.

HAND-MADE MAYONNAISE
Place 1 egg yolk in a mixing bowl and whisk in the dry mustard, seasoning
and white wine vinegar. Gradually add the oil, whisking continuously until
the mixture becomes thick and glossy.

FLAVORINGS
Various flavorings can be added to the basic mayonnaise mixture at the end
of preparation. To serve with poultry, stir in 3 tablespoons of chopped fresh
tarragon. To serve with fish, stir in either 3 tablespoons of chopped fresh dill
or 3 tablespoons of finely chopped capers.

TOMATO SAUCE

A tomato-based sauce is one of the most useful recipes in a lactose-free diet as it can be used as a substitute for most creamy or cheese sauces and is delicious with pasta, vegetables, meat or fish dishes.

1 Heat the oil in a saucepan over medium heat and add the shallots and garlic. Cook them for 5 minutes, stirring occasionally to prevent them becoming browned.

2 Add the tomatoes and tomato purée to the pan and stir to mix all the ingredients. Slowly bring the mixture to a boil. Reduce the heat and simmer for 15 minutes until the tomatoes are soft and the sauce is thick. Stir in the chopped basil and season with salt and black pepper.

¼ cup olive oil

2 shallots, peeled and chopped

2 cloves garlic, peeled and chopped

3½ pounds ripe tomatoes, skinned, seeded and chopped

3 tablespoons tomato purée

4 tablespoons chopped fresh basil

Salt and black pepper to taste

Makes approximately 3½–4 cups

STOCKS

Stock can be refrigerated in a plastic container for three days or can be frozen (omitting the seasoning) in ice cube trays for up to two months.

FISH STOCK
Place ¾ pound of fish heads and bones in a large saucepan with 1 peeled and halved onion, a small bunch of fresh parsley sprigs and 3 slices of lime. Cover with cold water and slowly bring to a boil. Skim the surface using a small sieve to remove any impurities, then reduce the heat and simmer for 10–15 minutes. Strain, discard the fish bones and onion and use the liquid as required.

CHICKEN STOCK
Place 1 pound of chicken carcass in a saucepan with ¼ pound of chopped mixed vegetables, 1 bouquet garni, 4 black peppercorns and 3 cups of cold water. Bring to a boil, then cover and simmer for 60–90 minutes, skimming the surface during cooking. Strain and use the liquid as required.

VEGETABLE STOCK
Place 1 pound of chopped vegetables, such as onions, carrots and celery into a saucepan with 6 cups of cold water. Bring to a boil, then cover and simmer for 50 minutes. Strain, gently pressing the vegetables to extract all the flavor.

LAMB STOCK
Preheat the oven to 450°F, 230°C, gas mark 8. Place 2 pounds of lamb bones in a roasting pan and brown in the oven for 15 minutes. Add 1 chopped carrot, 1 chopped stick of celery and 1 chopped leek. Roast for 15 minutes, then transfer to a saucepan with 6 cups of cold water, 1 bouquet garni, 4 black peppercorns and 1 tablespoon of tomato purée. Bring to a boil, then cover and simmer for 2 hours, skimming the surface during cooking. Strain and use as required.

5

Food for Kids

TOMATOES
_____

FISH
_____

POULTRY
_____

BEEF
_____

PORK
_____

DESSERTS

Avocado & Tuna Stuffed Tomatoes

4 large tomatoes

2 ripe avocados, stoned, peeled and cut into chunks

Grated rind and juice of ½ lemon

2 scallions, trimmed and sliced

6-ounce can tuna, drained

⅔ cups plain soy yogurt

Salt and black pepper to taste

4 slices bread

Fresh chives to garnish

Serves 4

A delicious mix of tuna chunks, avocados and soy yogurt is used to fill tomatoes in this attractive meal-in-one (see below), which tastes as good as it looks! The versatile filling can also be stirred into cooked, cooled pasta and served as a salad.

1 Slice the tops off the tomatoes and discard. Carefully scoop out the tomato seeds with a small metal spoon, leaving a tomato "shell."

2 Stir the avocado chunks and lemon juice together in a mixing bowl, taking care not to mash the avocados. Then fold in the lemon rind, scallions, tuna chunks and yogurt. Season with salt and black pepper. Place the tomato shells on a chopping board and fill them carefully with the tuna and avocado mixture.

3 Cut the bread slices into circles which are slightly larger than the tomato shells and toast them under a preheated broiler until lightly browned on both sides. Place one on each serving plate and sit the filled tomatoes on the top. Serve immediately, sprinkled with a few snipped chives.

BACON AND COUSCOUS STUFFED TOMATOES

Slice the tops off the tomatoes and scoop out the seeds as instructed in the recipe opposite. Chop ½ pound (8–10 slices) of bacon into cubes.

Heat 1 tablespoon of olive oil in a skillet and add the cubed bacon. Cook over high heat for 5 minutes until the bacon is fairly crispy, then add 1 cup of diced zucchini and cook for a further 5 minutes until the zucchini begins to soften. Remove the bacon and zucchini from the heat and set aside.

Prepare ½ cup of couscous according to the packet instructions. Separate the grains with a fork, then mix in the bacon and zucchini and stir until all the ingredients are combined. Season with salt and black pepper to taste. Spoon the mixture into the tomato shells, place on toasted bread circles and serve.

MUSHROOM AND TOFU STUFFED TOMATOES

Preheat the oven to 375°F, 190°C, gas mark 5. Slice the tops off the tomatoes and scoop out the seeds as instructed in the recipe opposite.

Wash and slice ¼ pound of mixed mushrooms. Heat 1 tablespoon of olive oil in a skillet and add the sliced mushrooms. Cook them over medium heat for 5 minutes until they begin to soften. Add ⅔ cup of finely cubed tofu and cook for a further 3 minutes until the tofu is heated through. Finally, stir in 1 tablespoon of sesame seeds and mix well.

Spoon the mushroom and tofu mixture into the tomato shells and bake in the preheated oven for 10 minutes, until the tofu is cooked through. Serve hot, placed on toasted bread circles.

TOMATO CATHERINE WHEELS

Filo pastry (see page 54) is tightly rolled with a filling of sun-dried tomato paste. The rolls are then sliced to reveal a pretty spiral pattern. Tomato Catherine Wheels look lovely arranged on a platter and are the ideal snack for children's parties—the grown-ups like them too, with drinks. They also make a great substitute for croutons when served with soups.

1¾ ounces filo pastry, 3 sheets measuring approximately 12 x 16-inches

½ cup sun-dried tomato paste

1 egg, beaten to glaze

Mayonnaise to serve (see page 76)

¼ pound cooked ham or chicken, chopped (optional)

Makes 20–25

1   Preheat the oven to 375°F, 190°C, gas mark 5. Lay the sheets of filo pastry flat on a work surface. Spread each sheet with a thin layer of the sun-dried tomato paste. Then, tightly roll up each sheet of filo pastry from the wider edge like a jelly roll. Keep the unused filo pastry under a damp cloth.

2   Cut each roll into ½ inch-thick slices using a sharp knife and place them on a large baking sheet. Brush the top of each slice with some beaten egg. Bake in the preheated oven for 8 minutes until the pastry is golden brown and cooked through and the filling is hot.

3   Place the filo rolls on a large platter and serve with a dip of ready-made or home-made Mayonnaise (see page 76) in a separate bowl. If desired, these rolls can be topped with finely chopped ham or chicken.

FISH CAKES WITH TOMATO SALSA

FOR THE FISH CAKES

1¾ pounds large potatoes, peeled and chopped

1¾ pounds haddock fillet

4 black peppercorns

1 bay leaf

3 tablespoons chopped fresh chervil or parsley

Salt and black pepper to taste

2 large eggs

1½ cups fresh white breadcrumbs

3 tablespoons olive oil

FOR THE TOMATO SALSA

4 medium-ripe tomatoes, seeded and chopped

1 red bell pepper, seeded and chopped

4 sticks celery, trimmed and chopped

3 tablespoons olive oil

Makes 12

My own children, Alicia and Sophie, love these haddock fish cakes which are served with a chunky tomato salsa (see right), and are far tastier than store-bought fish sticks. In fact, they are so popular with the kids that I have deliberately increased the measures of the recipe in order to produce a large quantity of fish cakes, so that half can be enjoyed immediately while the rest can be frozen for another day. Allow 1–2 fish cakes per child.

1   To prepare the fish cakes, place the potatoes in a saucepan, cover with water and bring to a boil. Reduce the heat and simmer for 15 minutes until the potatoes are tender. Drain the potatoes, then mash until smooth.

2   Meanwhile, place the haddock fillet in a large shallow saucepan and add the peppercorns and bay leaf. Cover with boiling water and cook the fish over gentle heat for 5 minutes until the flesh flakes easily. Once cooked, drain the fish and discard the bones and skin.

3   Coarsely flake the fish and place it in a large bowl. Mix in the mashed potato and chervil or parsley and season with salt and black pepper. Mold the mixture into 12 round patties using lightly floured hands to prevent the potato and fish mixture from becoming sticky.

4   Place the breadcrumbs in a shallow container. Dip each fish cake first into the beaten egg and then into the breadcrumbs, turning them until they are evenly coated. Chill the fish cakes in the refrigerator for 30 minutes. Alternatively, wrap them in aluminum foil and freeze them at this point.

5   When ready to serve, heat the oil in a large skillet and add the fish cakes. Cook over medium heat for 3–4 minutes on both sides until golden and cooked through. Do this in small batches, keeping the cooked fish cakes warm in the oven while cooking the next batch.

6   To prepare the tomato salsa, place the chopped tomatoes, bell pepper and celery in a bowl and mix together. Drizzle in the olive oil and stir until all the vegetables are coated in oil. Serve the fish cakes hot with the tomato salsa and a green salad.

COD FISH CAKES WITH CUCUMBER SALSA

A cod fillet may be used as a substitute for the haddock in the recipe above. Cod fish cakes work well with a cucumber salsa—replace the tomatoes in the salsa recipe with a 5-inch piece of seeded and chopped cucumber.

CHICKEN FINGERS & FRENCH FRIES

FOR THE CHICKEN FINGERS

I large egg

½ teaspoon turmeric

⅓ cup fresh wholewheat breadcrumbs

⅓ cup coarse oatmeal

2 boneless, skinless chicken breast halves (about ¾ pound)

4 tablespoons sunflower oil

FOR THE FRENCH FRIES

I pound large potatoes

Sunflower oil for frying

Coarse sea salt to taste

Serves 4 (makes I pound)

Both the chicken fingers and the French fries (see above) can be prepared up to four hours ahead of cooking: coat the chicken strips in breadcrumbs and chill in the refrigerator; slice the potatoes into matchsticks and leave in a saucepan covered with cold water.

1 Preheat the oven to 400°F, 200°C, gas mark 6. To prepare the fingers, beat the egg with the turmeric in a shallow bowl and set aside. Then mix together the breadcrumbs and oatmeal in a separate bowl and set aside.

2 Slice the chicken breasts very thinly using a sharp knife. Dip the chicken strips into the egg and turmeric mixture, turning them frequently to coat the chicken thoroughly. Then dip the chicken strips into the breadcrumbs and oatmeal mixture, turning until each piece is evenly coated.

3 Place the coated chicken on a baking sheet and drizzle over the sunflower oil. Bake in the preheated oven for 15 minutes until the chicken is crisp on the outside and cooked through.

4 To prepare the French fries, cut the potatoes into long matchsticks. Rinse in cold water and pat dry with paper towel. Heat the oil in a heavy-based pan or deep-fat fryer and add the matchstick potatoes. Cook over high heat for 2–3 minutes, in batches if necessary. Drain thoroughly on paper towel and serve immediately with the chicken fingers and a dollop of mayonnaise.

BEEF MEATBALLS WITH GOOEY CENTERS

Kids of all ages love these delicious meatballs which are cooked in tomato sauce and contain a lovely surprise. If people proclaim that dairy-free cooking is unexciting, I serve this dish to prove them wrong!

FOR THE MEATBALLS

3 tablespoons sunflower oil

1 onion, peeled and finely chopped

1 clove garlic, peeled and crushed

1½ pounds ground beef

3 tablespoons chopped fresh parsley

Salt and black pepper to taste

1 ounce soy cheese

FOR THE SAUCE

1 tablespoon sunflower oil

1 onion, peeled and finely chopped

1⅓ cups canned tomatoes, blended until smooth in a blender

Salt and black pepper to taste

Serves 4

1 To prepare the meatballs, heat the oil in a skillet and add the onion and garlic. Cook over medium heat for 5 minutes until softened. Remove from the heat and leave to cool.

2 Mix the cooled onions into the ground beef in a bowl and add the parsley, salt and black pepper. Do this with your hands to ensure the ingredients are evenly mixed. Cut the cheese into 20 cubes and, using lightly floured or damp hands (to prevent the mixture becoming sticky), surround each cube of cheese with some ground beef and mold into 20 balls.

3 To prepare the sauce, heat the oil in a skillet and add the onion. Cook over medium heat for 5 minutes until softened, not browned. Remove from the pan and set aside. Now cook the meatballs in batches in the same pan over high heat for 10 minutes until browned. Remove and set aside.

4 Return the onions to the pan with the sieved tomatoes and bring to a boil. Add the meatballs and simmer for 10 minutes until heated through. Season with salt and black pepper and serve with boiled rice and peas.

POLENTA-TOPPED PIE

Polenta is the staple carbohydrate of northern Italy. It can be cooked in many ways—here, it tastes great as a topping for ground beef.

1 tablespoon olive oil

1 large onion, peeled and finely chopped

2 cloves garlic, peeled and chopped

2 pounds ground beef chuck

15-ounce can chopped tomatoes

⅔ cup canned tomatoes, blended until smooth in a blender

⅔ cup beef stock

1 teaspoon dried parsley

Salt and black pepper to taste

1¼ cups instant polenta

Serves 6

1 Preheat the oven to 375°F, 190°C, gas mark 5. Heat the olive oil in a large skillet and add the onion and garlic. Cook over medium heat for 5 minutes until softened, not browned. Then stir in the ground beef chuck and cook for 10–15 minutes until browned, stirring frequently to prevent it sticking to the base of the pan.

2 Stir in the chopped tomatoes, sieved tomatoes and stock and then bring to a boil, stirring occasionally. Then simmer for 15 minutes until the meat is cooked through. Add the parsley and season with salt and black pepper.

3 Cook the polenta according to the packet instructions. Season with salt and black pepper. Spoon the beef mixture into a large ovenproof dish, top with the polenta mixture and smooth out the surface. Bake in the preheated oven for 25 minutes until the top is golden brown. Remove the pie from the oven and serve immediately with steamed broccoli.

Spaghetti Carbonara

1 large egg

4 teaspoons all-purpose flour

¾ cup and 1 tablespoons plain soy yogurt

1 tablespoon olive oil

1 clove garlic, peeled and chopped

1 onion, peeled and chopped

½ pound Canadian bacon, chopped

½ pound dried spaghetti or pasta shapes

Salt and black pepper to taste

3 tablespoons chopped fresh
flat-leaf parsley

Serves 4

This popular Italian dish is traditionally made with a sauce of cream, eggs, Parmesan cheese and bacon. This lactose-free version uses flour and soy yogurt in place of the cream and cheese, and is just as tasty (see right). Add cooked fresh green peas to the spaghetti with the bacon and onions for extra color if desired.

1   Beat the egg and flour together in a bowl until smooth. Gradually stir in the yogurt and set aside.

2   Heat the oil in a large skillet and add the garlic and onion. Cook over medium heat until they soften and begin to brown. Add the bacon and continue to cook for 5 minutes until the bacon begins to brown.

3   Meanwhile, bring a large saucepan of lightly salted water to a boil. Add the dried spaghetti and cook according to packet instructions. Drain the spaghetti and place it back into the pan to keep hot.

4   Add the bacon and onion mixture and the egg and yogurt mixture to the hot spaghetti and mix well. Season with salt and black pepper and serve sprinkled with parsley.

Ham & Egg Packages

2 large eggs

9 ounces filo pastry, 12–16 sheets
measuring approximately 12 x 16 inches

1 tablespoon sunflower oil

10–12 ounces cooked ham, cubed

3 tablespoons plain soy yogurt

3 tablespoons snipped fresh chives

1 egg, beaten, to glaze

Serves 8

Ham and eggs make a wonderful combination and they are especially delicious wrapped in filo pastry (see page 54) and then baked. For a more exotic filo package, replace the ham with cooked shrimp.

1   Preheat the oven to 425°F, 220°C, gas mark 7. Bring a small pan of water to a boil and add the eggs. Reduce the heat and simmer for 6–10 minutes. Remove the eggs and leave them under cold running water to cool. When cool enough to handle, peel and quarter them and set aside.

2   Layer 3–4 sheets of filo pastry, brushing each layer with oil before adding the next so that the sheets stick together. When you have 4 rectangles of layered pastry sheets, cut the rectangles in half to leave 8 squares. Keep the unused filo pastry covered with a damp cloth. Divide the cubed ham into 8 and place 1 portion on each square with a quarter of hard-boiled egg. Make sure you place this filling in the middle of each square, leaving enough of the edges free to be folded over the mixture.

3   Mix the yogurt and chives in a bowl and place a dollop of this mixture on top of the ham and egg. Brush a little beaten egg around the edge of the pastry. Fold the edges of the pastry over the filling to make packages. Arrange the packages on a baking sheet, brush with beaten egg and bake in the oven for 5–8 minutes until golden brown. Serve with a green salad.

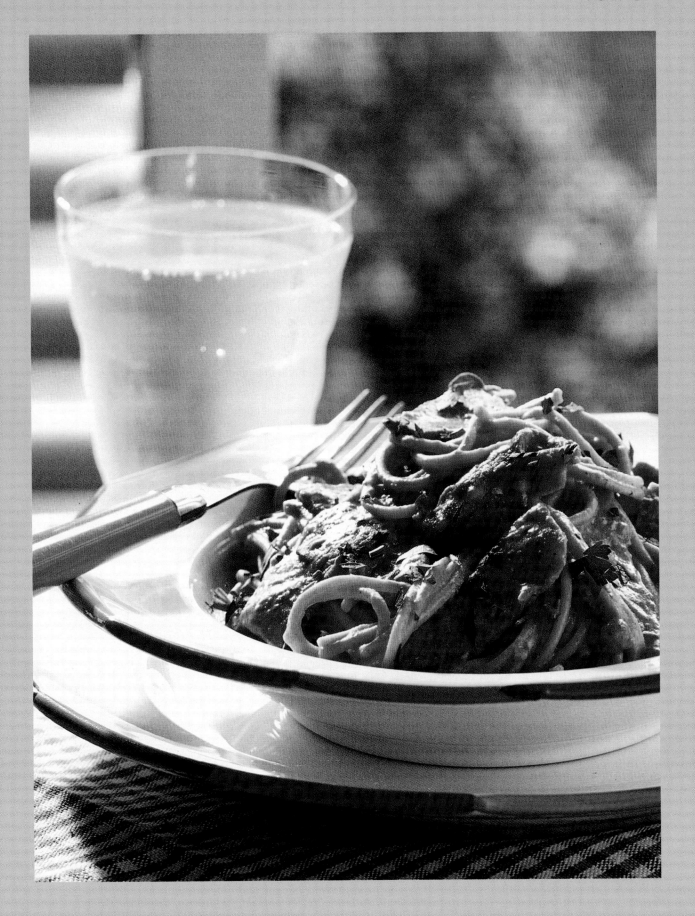

PORK & APPLE BURGERS

A platter of these tempting mini burgers (see left)—made with a blend of pork, apples and mushrooms—always goes down well at children's parties. To freeze these burgers, prepare and shape them as described, then open-freeze them on sheets of plastic wrap. Once frozen, transfer them to a rigid container. When ready to use, allow them to thaw completely on a wire rack for at least two hours, then cook as described below.

1 pound ground pork

2 apples, cored and grated

¼ pound button mushrooms, finely chopped

Salt and black pepper to taste

3 tablespoons olive oil

20 small dinner bread rolls

3 heads romaine lettuce, washed and chopped

Tomato Relish to serve (see below)

Serves 10

1   Mix together the ground pork, grated apple and chopped mushrooms in a large mixing bowl and season with plenty of salt and black pepper. Blend well, using your hands if necessary, to ensure that all the ingredients are thoroughly combined.

2   Divide the pork mixture into 20 portions and mold into even-sized patties with lightly floured or dampened hands (to prevent the mixture becoming sticky). Place the burgers in a shallow dish, cover with plastic wrap and chill in the refrigerator for 30 minutes or freeze as described above.

3   Heat the oil in a large skillet and add the mini burgers. Cook over high heat for 5 minutes on each side until browned and cooked through. Do this in batches if necessary.

4   Cut the bread rolls in half and arrange the bases on a large serving plate. Spread half a teaspoon of Tomato Relish (see below) on each roll and then add a cooked burger. Place the other half of the roll over the top of the burger with the chopped lettuce, and serve.

VEGETARIAN BURGERS

Replace the ground pork with 1 pound of dry patty mix blended with 1 egg and replace the apples with 3 finely sliced scallions. Use these ingredients and prepare the burgers as described in the recipe above.

TOMATO RELISH

Peel, seed and chop 1 pound of ripe tomatoes. Heat 1 tablespoon of olive oil in a saucepan and add the tomatoes with 1 chopped stick of celery and 2 peeled and chopped shallots. Cook the vegetables over medium heat for 10 minutes until softened. Leave to cool before serving.

PIZZA WITH PORK & CORN

These mini pizzas topped with fresh tomato sauce, succulent pork and vegetables are marvellous for children's suppers. Pitas contain no dairy products, so make the perfect cheats' pizza base!

1 Preheat the oven to 400°F, 200°C, gas mark 6. Arrange the mini pitas side-by-side on a large baking sheet.

2 Heat 3 tablespoons of the oil in a saucepan and add the onion and garlic. Cook over high heat until the onion is softened, not browned.

3 Add the tomatoes to the pan and stir well. Increase the heat and bring the mixture to a boil. Continue to boil for 10 minutes until the tomato sauce is thick, stirring frequently to prevent the mixture sticking to the base of the pan. Season with salt and black pepper.

4 Heat the remaining oil in a skillet and add the chopped pork tenderloin. Cook over medium heat for 8–10 minutes, stirring frequently until the pork is browned and cooked through.

5 Spread the tomato sauce on the pitas and arrange the cooked pork, sliced pepper and the corn kernels on top. Bake in the preheated oven for 8–10 minutes until the topping is piping hot and the pitas are browned around the edges.

4 mini pitas

⅓ cup sunflower oil

1 onion, peeled and chopped

2 cloves garlic, peeled and crushed

15-ounce can chopped tomatoes

Salt and black pepper to taste

¼ pound pork tenderloin, coarsely chopped

1 green bell pepper, seeded and sliced

¼ cup corn kernels

Serves 4

HONEY SAUSAGES & MASHED POTATOES

Sausages roasted with honey and shallots and served with rich mash make the perfect winter warmer for your kids. Or sprinkle the sausages with toasted sesame seeds and watch them disappear at a drinks party.

1 Preheat the oven to 400°F, 200°C, gas mark 6. To prepare the sausages, place them in a large roasting pan with the shallots. Drizzle the honey over the top and stir until the sausages and onions are well coated.

2 Place the pan in the preheated oven and roast the sausages and shallots for 20 minutes until "sticky," golden and cooked through. Stir the mixture once or twice during cooking to ensure the sausages cook evenly and remain coated in honey.

3 Place the potatoes in a large saucepan and cover with cold water. Bring to a boil, reduce the heat and simmer for 15 minutes until soft. Drain, return to the pan and mash with the oil until smooth. Stir in the parsley and season with salt and black pepper. Serve immediately with the sausages.

FOR THE SAUSAGES

12 cocktail sausages

2 shallots, peeled and sliced into rings

⅓ cup honey

FOR THE MASHED POTATOES

¾ pound potatoes, peeled and chopped

3 tablespoons olive oil

3 tablespoons chopped fresh parsley

Salt and black pepper to serve

Serves 4

BAKED MARMALADE STEAMED PUDDINGS

Individual steamed puddings are baked in a bain-marie (a hot water bath) here, making them very light and fluffy. Grapefruit marmalade is used for the topping but you could also try fruit preserves.

FOR THE PUDDINGS

Sunflower or peanut oil for greasing

¾ cup and 2 tablespoons vegetable shortening

⅔ cup raw sugar (demerara)

3 large eggs

¾ cup ground almonds, sifted

I cup self-rising flour, sifted

9 tablespoons grapefruit marmalade

I teaspoon ground cardamom

1 Preheat the oven to 375°F, 190°C, gas mark 5. Grease 6 individual ¾ cup pudding molds or ramekins with sunflower or peanut oil.

2 Beat together the vegetable shortening and the sugar in a bowl until light and fluffy. Beat in the eggs, then fold in the sifted almonds and flour.

3 Place 1½ tablespoons of grapefruit marmalade in the base of each pudding mold. Pour over the sponge mixture and sprinkle the top with cardamom. Place the molds in a roasting pan that is half filled with boiling water. Bake for 25 minutes until risen and golden.

4   To prepare the orange glaze, place the superfine sugar in a small saucepan. Carefully peel the oranges, holding them over the pan as you peel to catch any juice. Segment the oranges and set aside. Add 6 tablespoons of cold water to the pan and heat gently until the sugar dissolves. Bring to a boil, then reduce the heat and simmer for 5 minutes. Add the orange segments and heat for a further 2 minutes.

5   Remove the puddings from the oven. Then run a sharp knife between the puddings and the molds (if necessary) and carefully turn them out on to serving plates. Drizzle with the hot orange glaze to serve.

FOR THE ORANGE GLAZE

⅔ cup superfine sugar

3 oranges

Makes 6

Chocolate Bread Pudding

This dairy-free version of Bread and Butter Pudding uses slices of Cinnamon Swirl Loaf and home-made Chocolate Sauce.

1   Place a roasting pan, half filled with water, in the oven and preheat the oven to 350°F, 180°C, gas mark 4. Grease a 1-quart baking dish with oil.

2   Spread the slices of Cinnamon Swirl Loaf (see page 118) with margarine and cut into triangles. Arrange in the prepared dish, margarine-side-up, overlapping if necessary. Pour over the Chocolate Sauce (see page 97) and press the loaf down gently. Leave to stand for 15 minutes.

3   Sprinkle the pudding with sugar and place the dish in the pan containing the hot water. Bake in the oven for 25 minutes until the sauce has just set.

Oil for greasing

8 slices Cinnamon Swirl Loaf (see page 118) or cinnamon-raisin bread

¼ cup non-dairy margarine for spreading

1 cup Chocolate Sauce (see page 97)

3 tablespoons raw sugar (demerara), available from gourmet stores

Serves 4

Oat Bars

These fruity and nutritious biscuits are bursting with oats, nuts and dried fruit. They are easy to make and perfect for packed lunches.

1   Preheat the oven to 325°F, 170°C, gas mark 3. Grease a 8-inch square pan with oil and line the bottom and sides with wax paper.

2   Place the vegetable shortening and brown sugar in a saucepan and heat gently until the shortening melts and the sugar dissolves—be careful not to burn the mixture. Add the oats, walnuts, raisins and dried apricots and stir until all the ingredients are combined. Press the mixture into the pan.

3   Bake the mixture in the preheated oven for 40 minutes until golden. Remove from the oven and leave to cool for 5 minutes, then mark into squares. Leave the oat bars in the pan to cool and set. Once cool, separate the squares and store them in an airtight container for 4 days or freeze for up to 1 month and thaw for 3 hours on a wire rack before serving.

Oil for greasing

¾ cup vegetable shortening

¾ cup and 1 tablespoon packed light brown sugar

4⅔ cups rolled oats

½ cup chopped walnuts

⅓ cup raisins

½ cup chopped ready-to-eat apricots

Makes 16 squares

MINI PLUM CRISPS

These crisps combine juicy cooked plums with an oaty crisp topping and are made in individual ramekins, which is the perfect amount for a child. They can also be frozen, uncooked, for one month.

1 Preheat the oven to 375°F, 190°C, gas mark 5. To prepare the filling, place the plums and sugar in a large saucepan and heat gently for 10 minutes until the sugar dissolves and the fruit is soft.

2 To prepare the crisp topping, mix the flour and rolled oats together in a bowl. Rub in the shortening with your fingertips until the mixture resembles fine breadcrumbs. Then stir in the brown sugar.

3 Divide the filling between 6 individual 3-ounce ramekins (or 1 large 1-quart dish) and top with the crisp mixture. Bake in the preheated oven for 15–20 minutes (20–25 minutes for 1 large dish) and serve immediately.

FOR THE FILLING

1½ pounds plums, pitted and quartered

½ cup packed light brown sugar

FOR THE CRISP TOPPING

1 cup all-purpose flour

⅓ cup rolled oats

⅓ cup and 1 tablespoon vegetable shortening

⅓ cup packed light brown sugar

Serves 6

FRUITY MILK SHAKES

Soy milk, yogurt and red berries are blended to create these nutritious fruity shakes. Fresh or frozen raspberries or strawberries are the best berries to use as they give delicious flavor and vivid color (see left).

Place the fruit and confectioners' sugar in a food processor. Blend until a purée is formed then, with the motor still running, add the soy milk and yogurt. (Alternatively, pass the fruits through a sieve to purée and whisk in the soy milk and yogurt.) Divide the mixture between 2 tall glasses and add the crushed ice to serve.

½ pound red berries

3 tablespoons confectioners' sugar

1 cup soy milk or oat milk

1 cup plain soy yogurt

8 ice cubes, crushed

Makes 2

CHOCOLATE CHIP MINI MUFFINS

Chocolate chip muffins (see left) make an ideal snack for children and adults alike. Try adding chopped dried mango, golden raisins or toasted hazelnuts in place of the chocolate chips for an alternative.

1 Preheat the oven to 425°F, 220°C, gas mark 7. Line mini muffin tins with mini paper liners.

2 Sift together the flour, baking powder and superfine sugar in a bowl. Beat together the egg, oat milk and cooled shortening in a separate bowl and stir into the flour mixture with the chocolate chips until well combined.

3 Spoon into the paper liners and bake in the oven for 15 minutes until risen and golden brown. Serve warm.

1¼ cups self-rising flour

1 teaspoon baking powder

6 tablespoons superfine sugar

1 large egg

¾ cup oat milk

½ cup and 1 tablespoon vegetable shortening, melted

¾ cup bittersweet chocolate chips

Makes 30

6 Desserts

Blueberry Rice Pudding

Dried blueberries give this creamy rice pudding its striking purple color (see above). For an equally delicious alternative, use dried cranberries, but add extra sugar or a few raisins to sweeten the dish.

¼ cup short-grain rice

2 tablespoons superfine sugar

3⅓ cups coconut milk

2 cups fresh blueberries or ¾ cup dried blueberries

⅓ cup plain soy yogurt

Shredded coconut to serve

Serves 4

1 Place the rice and sugar in a large saucepan and mix well to combine. Stir in the coconut milk and heat gently for 3–4 minutes, stirring occasionally until the sugar dissolves.

2 Add the blueberries and continue to cook gently for a further 30 minutes, stirring frequently until the rice is tender and has absorbed all the coconut milk. The mixture should be thick and creamy. Divide the rice pudding between 4 pudding bowls and top each portion with a tablespoonful of plain soy yogurt. Sprinkle with the shredded coconut to serve.

BAKED CHOCOLATE PUDDINGS WITH CHOCOLATE SAUCE

These individual puddings are wonderfully light due to the addition of egg whites. A delicious chocolate sauce is poured over the sponges to serve, soaking into them to create a rich and highly chocolatey dessert.

1   Preheat the oven to 375°F, 190°C, gas mark 5. Grease 6 individual 6-ounce ramekins, pudding or oval dariole molds with oil. Then use a little of the grated chocolate to coat the inside of each mold with a fine layer.

2   To prepare the chocolate puddings, melt the remaining grated chocolate in a heatproof bowl placed over a saucepan of simmering water. Beat the shortening and egg yolks with half the sugar in a separate bowl until thick and creamy, then stir in the melted chocolate.

3   Sift the flour and cocoa powder into the chocolate mixture and fold it in. Whisk the egg whites in a separate bowl until stiff. Gradually whisk the remaining sugar into the egg whites, then fold into the chocolate mixture. Divide the mixture between the prepared molds and bake in the oven for 15 minutes until well risen and springy. Run a knife between the puddings and the molds (if necessary) and turn them out on to warmed serving dishes. Pour over the Chocolate Sauce (see below) to serve.

Oil for greasing

7 ounces bittersweet chocolate, finely grated

½ cup vegetable shortening

3 large eggs, separated

¾ cup and 2 tablespoons superfine sugar

2 tablespoons all-purpose flour

⅓ cup cocoa powder

2 cups Chocolate Sauce (see below)

Serves 6

CHOCOLATE SAUCE

Place 4 ounces of chopped bittersweet chocolate and 1⅔ cup of soy milk in a saucepan. Heat, stirring constantly until the chocolate melts. Mix 4 tablespoons of soy milk with 3 tablespoons each of cornstarch and granulated sugar. Whisk into the chocolate milk in the pan. Bring to a boil, reduce the heat and simmer for 3 minutes, stirring constantly until the sauce thickens. (Makes 2 cups.)

BAKED MINI PINEAPPLES

Baby pineapples are filled with fresh fruit and topped with meringue before being baked briefly, resulting in a light and warm fruit dessert.

1   Preheat the oven to 425°F, 220°C, gas mark 7. Slice the baby pineapples in half lengthwise and remove the flesh using a knife, keeping the skins intact. Chop the flesh into cubes and mix with the mango and strawberries.

2   Arrange the pineapple shells side-by-side on a baking sheet, spoon the fruit into the shells and pour over the kirsch. Whisk the egg whites until stiff but not dry, then gradually whisk in the superfine sugar until the mixture is stiff and glossy. Spoon or pipe this over the fruit to cover, then bake in the preheated oven for 5 minutes until the meringue is pale golden.

2 baby pineapples

1 large ripe mango, peeled and cubed

½ pound strawberries, hulled and halved

2 tablespoons kirsch

3 egg whites

¾ cup and 2 tablespoons superfine sugar

Serves 4

HOT FRUIT SOUFFLÉ WITH SLOE GIN-MACERATED FRUITS

FOR THE SOUFFLE

Oil for greasing

3½ tablespoons sunflower margarine

⅓ cup all-purpose flour

½ can concentrated frozen orange juice, defrosted (¾ cup once thawed)

¼ cup superfine sugar

3 tablespoons fresh orange juice

4 egg whites

FOR THE FRUITS

1 pound prepared mixed red berries, such as small strawberries, raspberries, cherries or red currants

⅓ cup sloe or damson gin or cassis

Fresh mint sprigs to decorate

Serves 4

Sloe gin-soaked fruits are served topped with a light orange soufflé in this tasty pudding. If you are unable to find sloe or damson gin then use cassis which is readily available. This dessert can be made using either fresh or frozen fruits and enjoyed all year.

1   Preheat the oven to 400°F, 200°C, gas mark 6. Grease a 1-quart (4-cup) soufflé dish with oil and coat it with superfine sugar, which helps the soufflé stick to the sides of the dish as it rises.

2   To prepare the soufflé, melt the margarine in a saucepan and stir in the flour. Remove the pan from the heat and gradually add the orange juice and ¾ cup water. Bring to a boil, stirring constantly. Reduce the heat and simmer for 1 minute until a smooth, thick orange paste is formed. Remove the pan from the heat and stir in the sugar and fresh orange juice.

3   Whisk the egg whites in a bowl until stiff, then gradually whisk them into the orange mixture. Pour this mixture into the prepared soufflé dish and bake in the oven for 15–20 minutes until golden and firm to touch.

4   Meanwhile, place a mixture of strawberries, raspberries, cherries and red currants in a single layer on 4 individual serving plates and pour over the sloe or damson gin. Leave to macerate for 15–20 minutes while the soufflé is cooking.

5   Remove the soufflé from the oven, divide it into 4 portions and spoon on top of the macerated fruits. Place a sprig of mint on each helping to serve.

HOT COFFEE SOUFFLÉ

Oil for greasing

2 tablespoons non-dairy margarine

1½ tablespoons all-purpose flour

½ cup soy milk

½ cup hot strong black coffee

4 large eggs, separated

¼ cup superfine sugar

Confectioners' sugar for dusting

Serves 4

This coffee soufflé uses ingredients found in most kitchen cupboards so is a marvelous standby for entertaining unexpected guests.

1   Preheat the oven to 375°F, 190°C, gas mark 5. Grease a 1-quart soufflé dish with oil. Melt the margarine in a saucepan and stir in the flour. Remove from the heat and gradually stir in the soy milk, then the coffee. Place the pan back on the heat and bring the sauce to a boil, stirring constantly, then simmer for 2 minutes. Remove from the heat and leave to cool.

2   Beat the egg yolks and sugar until thick and fold into the cooled coffee sauce. Whisk the egg whites in a bowl until stiff and fold into the coffee mixture. Spoon this mixture into the soufflé dish and place in a roasting pan half filled with boiled water. Bake in the oven for 40 minutes until well risen and just firm to touch. Dust with confectioners' sugar to serve.

SOUFFLÉED OMELETTE WITH CARAMELIZED ORCHARD FRUITS

This light and fluffy sweet souffléed omelette is very quick and easy to prepare and goes wonderfully well with a filling of fall fruits.

1 To prepare the sauce, place the apples and pears in a large saucepan and add the apricot preserves. Cook gently over low heat for 10 minutes until the fruits become soft. Stir in the Cointreau and set aside.

2 To prepare the soufflé, whisk the egg whites in a bowl until stiff but not dry. Beat the egg yolks with the vanilla sugar in a separate bowl until thick and creamy and fold into the whisked egg whites.

3 Preheat the broiler. Heat a non-stick omelette pan or small skillet over medium heat on the stovetop. Spoon the egg mixture into the pan and cook for 2 minutes until golden underneath. Place the pan under the preheated broiler for 2–3 minutes until the top is golden and puffy.

4 Using a palette knife make a small indentation along the center of the omelette, taking care not to cut all the way through. Spoon the fruit filling on to one half, fold the omelette over and carefully transfer to a serving plate. Sprinkle liberally with confectioners' sugar and cut in half to serve.

FOR THE SAUCE

2 apples, peeled, cored and sliced

2 pears, peeled, cored and sliced

3 tablespoons apricot preserves

1 tablespoon Cointreau

FOR THE SOUFFLÉED OMELETTE

3 large eggs, separated

3 tablespoons vanilla sugar (to prepare: store superfine sugar in a jar with a split vanilla pod for at least 2 weeks)

Sifted confectioners' sugar for sprinkling

Serves 2

BLUEBERRY CLAFOUTIS

Fresh blueberries baked with a dairy-free batter topping make a delicious change from the more traditional cherry clafoutis.

1 Preheat the oven to 425°F, 220°C, gas mark 7. Arrange the blueberries in a 1½-quart (4-cup) shallow oval dish.

2 Beat together the eggs, flour and superfine sugar in a bowl until smooth. Place the soy milk in a saucepan and heat it gently. Gradually whisk it into the egg mixture. Pour the batter over the blueberries and dot with the margarine. Bake in the preheated oven for 30 minutes until the batter is puffed and golden on top. Serve hot.

¾ pound (about 3 cups) fresh blueberries

3 large eggs

⅓ cup all-purpose flour

¼ cup superfine sugar

1¾ cup soy milk

1 tablespoon non-dairy margarine

Serves 4

CRÈME BRÛLÉE

This non-dairy version (see left) of the great French pudding (which is traditionally made with cream, eggs and sugar) is so delicious, you will keep coming back for more!

Grated rind of 1 orange
2 cups plain soy yogurt
½ pound raspberries
1 cup superfine sugar
Serves 6

1   Mix together the orange rind and yogurt in a bowl. Then gently fold in the raspberries, taking care not to crush them.

2   Preheat the broiler. Divide the raspberry and yogurt mixture between 6 individual ⅔-cup ramekins and carefully sprinkle the superfine sugar evenly over the top of each portion.

3   Place the ramekins under the broiler for 4–5 minutes, until the sugar caramelizes to a crunchy topping with a rich golden brown color. It is important to keep an eye on the ramekins to ensure the sugar browns evenly and does not burn.

4   Leave the Crème Brûlées to stand for a maximum of 30 minutes before serving—if they stand for any longer the caramel topping will soften.

TOFFEE BANANAS

Bananas are partially cooked in a "creamy" toffee sauce, then flamed with brandy to enhance the flavor. To impress your dinner guests, take the dessert to the table still flaming.

½ cup light brown sugar
¼ teaspoon cornstarch
⅔ cup soy yogurt
4 medium-sized bananas, peeled and halved
3 tablespoons brandy (optional)
Serves 4

1   Place the brown sugar with 2 tablespoons of cold water in a shallow skillet. Heat gently until the sugar dissolves.

2   Increase the heat and bring the mixture to a boil. Continue to cook for 3–5 minutes until the sugar begins to caramelize. Remove from the heat. Mix the cornstarch into the yogurt then pour into the pan. Return to the heat and whisk until the mixture thickens. (The addition of cornstarch should prevent the mixture from curdling.)

3   Arrange the bananas side-by-side in a single layer in the toffee mixture and return the pan to the heat. Cook gently for 8–10 minutes until heated through. Then, if desired, pour the brandy over the top and ignite it with a long match. Serve immediately.

WARM SPICED FRUIT COMPOTE

Dried fruits are gently cooked in cider with cinnamon to create this warming winter dessert. You can make this pudding more refined by adding red wine in place of cider or make it suitable for children by using fresh orange juice instead of alcohol.

1 pound ready-to-eat dried fruits, such as figs, apricots, prunes or apple rings

1 cinnamon stick, halved

6 cloves

1-inch piece preserved stem ginger, finely chopped

2⅓ cups hard cider

Grated rind and juice of 1 orange

1 tablespoon honey (or to taste)

Serves 6

1 Place the dried fruit in a large saucepan and add the cinnamon stick, cloves and ginger. Toss gently, pour over the cider and mix well.

2 Slowly bring the fruit mixture to a boil over medium heat. Add the orange rind and juice and the honey. Reduce the heat and simmer for 10 minutes until the fruit is very tender. Remove the pan from the heat and spoon the fruits into serving bowls. Serve warm with Coconut Ice Cream (see page 109). Alternatively, chill in the refrigerator and serve cold with a dollop of plain soy yogurt.

POACHED PEARS

Whole pears, as they are poached, absorb the bold flavors of sweet wine, aromatic spices, lemon and vanilla in this refreshing dessert (see left)—a perfect end to any meal. I find the best sweet wine to use is Barsac which is better value than Sauternes.

12 fl oz dessert wine

¾ cup superfine sugar

Thinly pared rind and juice of 1 lemon

1 cinnamon stick, halved

1 vanilla bean, split

6 green cardamom pods, lightly crushed

6 even-sized pears, such as Bartlett, peeled

Serves 6

1 Pour the dessert wine into a saucepan that is large enough for all the pears to lay on their sides. Add the superfine sugar, the lemon rind and juice, the cinnamon stick, the vanilla bean and the green cardamom pods. Heat gently until the sugar dissolves.

2 Slice the bases of the pears so that they stand upright. Place them in the pan on their sides and cook gently until the liquid just begins to simmer.

3 Cover the pan with a large sheet of wax paper and simmer for 25 minutes. Turn the pears over carefully, re-cover with the wax paper and simmer for a further 25 minutes until tender. Lift the pears from the pan using a slotted spoon and stand on a serving platter.

4 Boil the pear and wine liquid rapidly for 5 minutes, until syrupy and golden brown. Spoon the syrup over the pears and serve warm with plain soy yogurt.

FRESH FRUIT TERRINE

This fabulous dish consists of fresh fruits set in an orange juice jelly—ideal for summertime lunch parties.

1 Line a 7-cup terrine or loaf pan with plastic wrap. Pour the orange juice into a saucepan and heat until the liquid is just about to boil. Remove the pan from the heat, then add the gelatin crystals. Stir constantly until the gelatin dissolves completely. Leave to cool for 15 minutes.

2 Prepare the fruits—halve or quarter any large strawberries, peel and chop the mangoes and peaches and halve the grapes. Mix the fruits together and arrange them attractively in the prepared terrine.

3 Pour the orange juice over the fruits and chill in the refrigerator for at least 3 hours until set. Turn out on to a chilled plate and peel away the plastic wrap. Decorate the terrine with strawberries and fresh mint leaves.

2⅔ cups orange juice

4½ packets (¼-ounce each) unflavored gelatin

2 pounds mixed summer fruits, such as strawberries, blueberries, mangoes, peaches, green grapes or raspberries

¼ pound strawberries to decorate

Sprigs of fresh mint leaves to decorate

Serves 6–8

UPSIDE-DOWN FRUIT TART

Forget the calories for a moment and tuck into this tasty apricot and sponge tart, which is delicious served warm with plain soy yogurt.

1 Preheat the oven to 350°F, 180°C, gas mark 4. Lightly grease a 8-inch round cake pan with oil.

2 To prepare the filling, place the sugar in a heavy-based saucepan with ¼ cup of cold water. Heat gently until the sugar dissolves fully. Bring the mixture to a boil, then simmer gently for 3–5 minutes until it turns a golden color. Pour this caramel over the base of the prepared cake pan and arrange the apricot halves over the top so they set in the caramel.

3 To prepare the sponge, sift the flour into a bowl and with two knives used scissor-fashion cut in the shortening until the mixture resembles coarse crumbs. Stir in the beaten eggs and sugar using a wooden spoon. Spoon the mixture over the apricots and smooth out the surface.

4 Bake in the preheated oven for 30–35 minutes until the sponge is golden and springy to touch. Leave the cake to cool in the pan for 5 minutes, then turn it out on to a serving plate, so the fruit is on the top. Serve warm with plain soy yogurt.

FOR THE FILLING

Oil for greasing

¾ cup granulated sugar

2 pounds fresh apricots, halved and pitted

FOR THE SPONGE

1¼ cups self-rising flour

½ cup vegetable shortening

2 large eggs, beaten

2 tablespoons superfine sugar

Plain soy yogurt to serve

Serves 6

UPSIDE-DOWN PLUM TART
Replace the apricots with 2 pounds of pitted and halved plums. To prepare the sponge, add ½ teaspoon of cinnamon to the flour and replace the superfine sugar with 2 tablespoons light brown sugar. Cook as above.

Individual Summer Puddings

2 pounds fresh summer fruits such as red currants, black currants, strawberries, raspberries, cherries or blackberries, plus extra to serve

⅔ cup granulated sugar

1 tablespoon cassis or black currant cordial

12 slices white bread, medium-sliced, crusts removed

Mint leaves and white or red currants to serve

Serves 6

This classic English dessert of berries encased in juice-soaked molded bread is here made in individual portions (see right). These puddings can be enjoyed all year round—prepare and freeze them in the summer, when the fruit is fresh, then defrost and serve them in the winter.

1 Place all the fruit in a large saucepan with the sugar and cassis or black currant cordial. Heat gently for 5 minutes until the sugar dissolves and the fruit begins to soften. Remove from the heat and set aside.

2 Line 6 individual ⅔-cup molds or ramekins with the bread. Cut 6 slices of bread into quarters, and cut 12 small circles from the other 6 slices (if you can't get 2 circles from each slice, you will need a few extra slices). Cover the base of each mold with one of the circles, then use four of the bread squares to line the sides. Ensure the bread lines the molds entirely, with no gaps left between slices (if using metal molds, line them first with plastic wrap). Reserve the remaining 6 circles to cover the molds.

3 Divide the fruit mixture into 6 portions and spoon it into the bread-lined molds. Top each pudding with the reserved bread, then cover with plastic wrap. Sit a saucer over each mold and weight it down with a heavy can of food. Leave the puddings in the refrigerator to stand overnight.

3 Remove the weights and plastic wrap and turn the molds out on to serving plates. Garnish with mint leaves and white or red currants to serve.

Orchard Strudel

¾ pound Italian prune plums, pitted and chopped

¾ pound apples, peeled, cored and chopped

¾ pound pears, peeled, cored and chopped

¾ cup granulated sugar

6 ounces filo pastry, 10 sheets measuring approximately 12 x 16-inches

2 teaspoons ground nutmeg

1 cup soy yogurt, ¼ cup Calvados or orange juice and white or red currants to serve (optional)

Serves 6

Fresh plums, apples and pears are ideal for cooking in thin sheets of filo pastry (see page 56). A dried fruits mixture soaked in orange juice can be used as an alternative if fresh fruits are not available.

1 Preheat the oven to 375°F, 190°C, gas 5. Gently cook the fruit and sugar in a saucepan for 5 minutes until the sugar dissolves and the fruit softens.

2 Lay a sheet of filo pastry on a work surface and sprinkle with a little of the ground nutmeg. Top with another sheet of filo and repeat until all but 2 of the filo sheets have been used. Cover the remaining 2 sheets with a damp kitchen towel to prevent them from drying out.

3 Spoon the fruit along one edge of the pastry. Tuck in the ends and roll up the strudel loosely. Cut the reserved filo pastry into strips, scrunch them into rosettes and arrange them on top of the strudel. Place the strudel on a large baking sheet and bake in the preheated oven for 20 minutes until the pastry is golden. Serve sliced, with soy yogurt flavored with Calvados or orange juice, if desired, and garnish with white or red currants.

RASPBERRY ICE MERINGUE NEST

This impressive meringue nest filled with raspberry ice (see left) is a good dessert for making ahead of time—the meringue stays fresh in an airtight container for up to two weeks and the raspberry ice can be frozen for up to three months. The same amount of fresh blueberries or strawberries can be used instead of the raspberries as an alternative.

1　Preheat the oven to 225°F, 110°C, gas mark ¼. Line a baking sheet with parchment paper. In the center of the parchment draw a 9-inch circle using a pencil, then turn the paper over so that you can still clearly see the circle through the paper.

2　To prepare the meringue, whisk the egg whites until stiff but not dry and greatly increased in volume. Whisk in half the superfine sugar until the mixture is stiff and glossy. Then whisk in the remaining sugar, adding the vanilla extract with the last of the sugar.

3　Spread a 1½-inch thick layer of meringue on the parchment paper to fill the marked circle. Then spoon the remaining meringue mixture into a pastry bag fitted with a large star tip and carefully pipe a rim around the edge of the meringue circle. If you do not have a pastry bag, mold the meringue into ovals using 2 dessert spoons and sit the ovals around the edge of the meringue circle to form a wall. Bake the nest in the preheated oven for 2 hours until crisp and dry. Turn off the heat and leave the meringue to cool in the oven, then peel off the parchment paper.

4　To make the raspberry ice, heat the soy milk with the cinnamon stick in a large saucepan over low heat until the milk begins to steam, then remove from the heat and set aside.

5　Whisk the egg yolks, sugar and cornstarch in a large mixing bowl until pale, then gradually add the heated milk. Place the mixture in a saucepan and cook gently for 5 minutes, stirring constantly until slightly thickened. Remove from the heat and leave to cool. Strain the cooled custard through a sieve and place in a bowl. Stir in the soy yogurt.

6　Place the raspberries in a food processor and blend until puréed, then sieve the mixture, if wished—this removes all the seeds, producing a smoother purée. (Alternatively, if you do not have a food processor, pass the fresh raspberries through a sieve.)

7　Stir the raspberry purée into the custard mixture and pour into a rigid container. Freeze for 3 hours until the mixture begins to set. Remove the mixture from the freezer and beat until smooth. Then return to the freezer for 4–5 hours until the mixture is solid.

8　When ready to serve, place the meringue on a serving plate and fill with scoops of the raspberry ice. Decorate with fresh red currants, if desired.

FOR THE MERINGUE

3 egg whites

¾ cup and 2 tablespoons superfine sugar

1 teaspoon vanilla extract

FOR THE RASPBERRY ICE

1⅓ cups soy milk

1 cinnamon stick, broken

3 egg yolks

⅔ cup superfine sugar

1½ tablespoons cornstarch

1⅓ cups plain soy yogurt

½ pound fresh raspberries

Fresh red currants to decorate (optional)

Serves 8

MANGO SORBET

15-ounce can mango slices

1⅓ cups pure tropical fruit juice

3 egg whites

Serves 8

Sorbets are made from a basic mixture of sugar, water and egg whites flavored with fruit. I have used mango slices and tropical fruit drink in this refreshing low-fat dessert. If you are uncomfortable using raw eggs, simply omit the egg white and serve this as a granita (see below).

1 Drain the mango slices, place them in a food processor and blend until smooth. With the motor running, gradually add the tropical fruit juice and ⅔ cup cold water. (Alternatively, pass the mango slices through a sieve and whisk in the fruit juice and water.) Sieve into a freezerproof container then freeze for 2–3 hours until thick, slushy and almost set.

2 Place the partially frozen mango mixture in a food processor and blend until smooth or beat the mixture by hand.

3 Whisk the egg whites until stiff. Fold into the mango mixture then return to the freezer for 4–5 hours until solid. Scoop into bowls to serve.

MELON SORBET

For a delicious melon sorbet, use 2 pounds of either Cantaloupe or Honeydew melon. Remove the flesh and blend it in a food processor with the juice of 2 lemons and 2 cups of confectioners' sugar. Once the mixture is smooth, pour it into a shallow container and freeze until slushy. Process again, then return the mixture to the freezer for 4–5 hours until solid.

STRAWBERRY GRANITA

½ pound fresh strawberries

1 tablespoon confectioners' sugar

1⅓ cups sweet white wine

Serves 4

Granita, a popular Italian dessert, is simply frozen flavored liquid that is scraped with a fork to create its characteristic granular texture.

1 Place the strawberries in a food processor and blend until smooth. Sieve the purée to remove the seeds. Stir in the confectioners' sugar and sweet wine, place the mixture in a shallow tray and freeze for 4 hours until solid.

2 Scrape the frozen mixture with a fork to produce crystals, then spoon it into chilled glasses to serve.

TROPICAL GRANITA

Cut 6 passion fruits in half and scoop out the seeds using a spoon. Mix these with ⅔ cup each of orange juice and fresh mango juice. Strain, then freeze and scrape as described above.

COCONUT ICE CREAM WITH CURRIED FRUIT SALAD

This dairy-free ice cream is served with a warm, exotic mixture of spiced fruits. For extra flavor, puréed red fruits such as strawberries or raspberries, or the grated rind and juice of a lime can be added to the basic ice cream mixture.

1 To prepare the ice cream, place the coconut milk in a large saucepan and heat gently until it begins to bubble. Remove from the heat. Whisk together the eggs and sugar in a mixing bowl until pale. Continue to whisk while adding the heated coconut milk in a steady stream.

2 Leave the mixture to cool, stirring occasionally. Pour into a freezerproof container and freeze for 3 hours. Remove from the freezer and scoop the ice cream into a food processor. Process until smooth. Pour back into the freezerproof container and return to the freezer for 4–5 hours until solid.

3 To make the fruit salad, place the orange rind and juice in a saucepan with the coriander seeds, turmeric, cumin and sugar. Heat gently for 5 minutes until the sugar dissolves.

4 Add the prepared fruits to the pan and heat gently for 5 minutes until the fruits are soft and just cooked. Leave to cool. Divide the fruit mixture between 6 dessert bowls and top with a scoop of ice cream to serve.

FOR THE ICE CREAM

3⅓ cups dairy-free coconut milk

4 large eggs

7 tablespoons superfine sugar

FOR THE CURRIED FRUIT SALAD

Grated rind and juice of 1 large orange

2 teaspoons coriander seeds, crushed

1 teaspoon ground turmeric

1 teaspoon ground cumin

3 tablespoons superfine sugar

2 mangoes, peeled, stoned and sliced

1 pineapple, peeled, cored and sliced

¼ pound cape gooseberries, husk removed (or 2 starfruits, sliced)

Serves 6

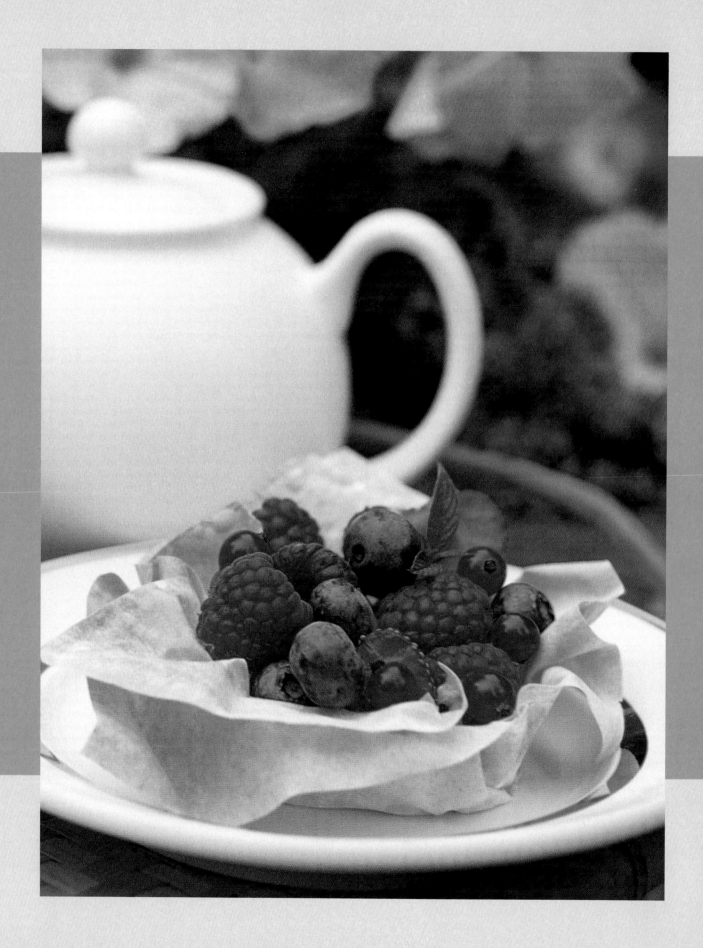

7

Cakes & Breads

CHESTNUT LOG

Chestnuts are in season between September and February—perfect for the holiday season, as is this rich chestnut sponge filled with a chocolate "cream." Decorate this cake with marrons glacés (chestnuts preserved in sweet syrup), if desired.

FOR THE SPONGE

Oil for greasing

4 large eggs

¾ cup superfine sugar

Few drops of vanilla extract

¼ cup cooked chestnuts, mashed

¾ cup all-purpose flour

1 tablespoon confectioners' sugar

FOR THE FILLING

3 ounces bittersweet chocolate, chopped

¾ cup plain soy yogurt

Confectioners' sugar and cocoa powder, sifted for dusting (optional)

Serves 8

1 Preheat the oven to 400°F, 200°C, gas mark 6. Grease a 12 x 8 x 1-inch jelly roll pan with oil and line the base with wax paper.

2 To prepare the cake, whisk the eggs, sugar and vanilla extract in a bowl until they are thick and creamy and a ribbon-like trail forms when the whisks are lifted from the mixture. Fold in the mashed chestnuts and flour.

3 Spoon the mixture into the prepared pan and bake in the preheated oven for 15 minutes until risen and springy to touch.

4 Lay a sheet of wax paper on a work surface and sift the confectioners' sugar over it. Remove the cake from the oven and carefully turn it out on to the wax paper. Leave to cool.

5 To prepare the filling, place the chocolate into a bowl and place over a saucepan of simmering water until melted. Remove from the heat, add the yogurt and beat until smooth. Spread the sponge with the chocolate mixture. Trim the edges of the sponge to neaten and, using the sheet of wax paper, roll the cake along the short edge to form a "log." Dust with sifted confectioners' sugar and cocoa powder to serve.

SPICY SYRUP CAKE

This moist maple syrup cake gets its spicy taste from chopped ginger. Lemon syrup makes a fitting topping.

Oil for greasing

¾ cup vegetable shortening

¾ cup light brown sugar

3 large eggs

¼ cup maple syrup

2 bulbs preserved stem ginger, each bulb weighing about ½ ounce, chopped

2½ cups self-rising flour

½ cup granulated sugar

Juice of 1 small lemon

Serves 8

1 Preheat the oven to 350°F, 180°C, gas mark 4. Lightly grease an 8-inch square cake pan with oil and line the base with wax paper.

2 Beat the shortening and the brown sugar in a mixing bowl until pale and fluffy. Then gradually beat in the eggs and maple syrup. Fold in the chopped ginger and the sifted flour. Spoon the mixture into the prepared tin and bake in the preheated oven for 1 hour.

3 Meanwhile place the sugar and lemon juice in a small saucepan. Cook gently over low heat until the sugar completely dissolves. Increase the heat and boil for 2 minutes. Remove the cake from the oven, turn out of the tin on to a plate, remove the lining paper and turn the right side up. Drizzle over the lemon syrup while the cake is still warm.

CARROT CAKE

The mashed bananas give this carrot cake (see above) its moist texture and delicious flavor. Keep it for four days in an airtight container or for one month in the freezer.

1 Preheat the oven to 350°F, 180°C, gas mark 4. Grease an 8-inch round cake pan with oil and line the base with wax paper.

2 Sift the flour and baking powder into a large bowl and mix in the brown sugar. Stir in the mashed bananas, grated carrot, beaten eggs and oil and beat until the mixture is runny. Pour the mixture into the prepared pan and bake in the preheated oven for 45–60 minutes. The cake is cooked when it shrinks from the edges of the pan, is firm to touch and golden in color.

3 Leave the cake to cool a little in the pan for 10 minutes before turning it out on to a wire rack. Remove the lining paper, turn the cake the right side up and allow to cool completely. Serve the cake cut into slices.

Oil for greasing

2¼ cups self-rising flour

1 teaspoon baking powder

¾ cup light brown sugar

2 medium-sized bananas, mashed

1 large carrot (weighing approximately 6 ounces), scrubbed and grated

3 large eggs, beaten

¾ cup sunflower oil

Serves 8

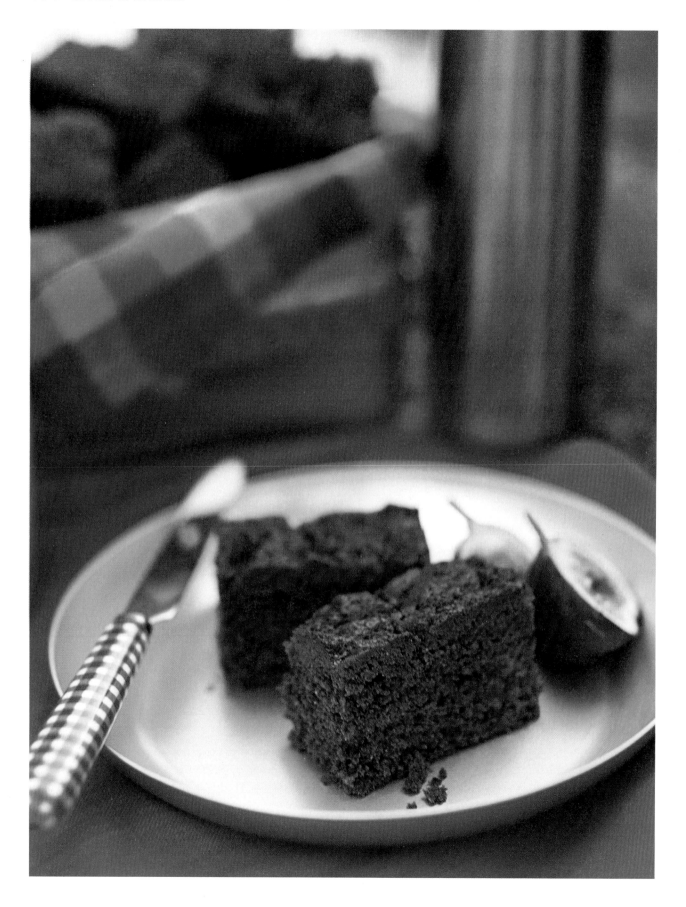

Chocolate Cake Bars

These Chocolate Cake Bars (see left) are deliciously gooey because they are made with oil rather than butter. It is best to leave them wrapped up for a day or two before serving as they become increasingly moist and tasty as they keep.

1 Preheat the oven to 350°F, 180°C, gas mark 4. Grease a 8-inch square cake pan with oil and line the base with wax paper.

2 Sift the flour with the baking powder into a large mixing bowl and stir in the brown sugar. Beat the cocoa and water mixture with the oil and the eggs in a separate bowl. Then beat this into the flour mixture until smooth. Finally, stir in the chopped chocolate.

3 Spoon the cake mixture into the prepared pan and bake in the preheated oven for 45–50 minutes until risen and cooked through. To test if the cake is cooked, insert a skewer into the middle of the cake—if it comes out clean the cake is cooked through. Turn out on to a wire rack to cool, remove the lining and cut into bars to serve.

Oil for greasing

2¼ cups self-rising flour

1 teaspoon baking powder

¾ cup light brown sugar

3 tablespoons cocoa powder, dissolved in an equal amount of boiling water

¾ cup sunflower oil

3 large eggs, beaten

2 ounces bittersweet chocolate, chopped

Makes 16 bars

Mocha Bars

To brighten up any mid-morning coffee break, serve these chocolate and coffee flavored bars. They can be frozen un-iced for up to two months.

1 Preheat the oven to 375°F, 190°C, gas mark 5. Grease a 7-inch square cake pan with oil and line the base with wax paper.

2 To prepare the cake, beat the eggs and sugar in a bowl until they are thick and creamy and a ribbon-like trail forms when the whisks are lifted from the mixture. Fold in the grated chocolate, sifted flour, then the coffee. Spoon the mixture into the prepared pan.

3 Bake in the preheated oven for 20 minutes until well risen and springy to touch. Leave the cake in the pan for 5 minutes before turning out on to a wire rack to cool.

4 To make the icing, mix the confectioners' sugar with the coffee and sufficient warm water to make a smooth icing. Melt the chocolate in a bowl placed over a saucepan of simmering water. Spoon the melted chocolate into a pastry bag fitted with a small plain tip.

5 Spread the coffee icing over the top of the cake. Decorate it by piping lines of chocolate horizontally across the icing, roughly ¾-inch apart. Using a skewer or cocktail stick, draw lines vertically through the chocolate in both directions to give a feather-like effect. Cut the cake into bars to serve.

FOR THE CAKE

Oil for greasing

4 large eggs

½ cup and 1 tablespoon superfine sugar

2 ounces bittersweet chocolate, finely grated

1 cup all-purpose flour, sifted

¼ cup strong, black filter coffee

FOR THE ICING

1¼ cups confectioners' sugar, sifted

1 tablespoon strong, black filter coffee

1 ounce bittersweet chocolate, chopped

Makes 14 bars

Simple Fruit Cake

Fruit cake is so often served just at Christmas or Easter, which is a great shame in my opinion. This delicious cake is perfect for serving at any time of the year.

Oil for greasing

1½ pounds dried mixed fruit, such as raisins, sultanas, mixed peel, chopped apricots or chopped prunes

1⅓ cups apple juice

¾ cups and 2 tablespoons vegetable shortening

¾ cup and 1 tablespoon light brown sugar

3 large eggs beaten

2½ cups self-rising flour

Serves 8

1 Preheat the oven to 300°F, 150°C, gas mark 2. Grease an 8-inch round cake pan with oil and line it with wax paper.

2 Place the mixed fruits in a large saucepan, pour over the apple juice and bring the mixture to a boil. Reduce the heat and simmer for 20 minutes. Remove the pan from the heat and leave to cool.

3 Cream the shortening and brown sugar in a large mixing bowl until pale. Gradually beat in the eggs, then fold in the flour and mixed fruit. Spoon the mixture into the prepared cake pan and bake in the oven for 3¼–3½ hours. Remove from the oven and leave in the pan for 5 minutes, then turn out on to a wire rack to cool.

Strawberry & Cardamom Roll

Adding cardamom to this jelly roll mixture produces a cake with a fascinating flavor which is complemented perfectly by strawberry soy yogurt and fresh strawberries.

FOR THE SPONGE

Oil for greasing

¼ cup green cardamom pods

⅔ cup all-purpose flour

3 large eggs

⅔ cup superfine sugar

FOR THE FILLING

Confectioners' sugar for dusting

⅔ cup strawberry-flavored soy yogurt

¼ pound strawberries, hulled and chopped

Serves 6

1 Preheat the oven to 400°F, 200°C, gas mark 6. Grease a 12 x 8 x ¾-inch jelly roll tin with oil and line it with wax paper.

2 Remove the cardamom seeds from the pods and crush them coarsely in a mortar with a pestle. Sift the flour into a bowl and set aside.

3 Whisk the eggs and the sugar in a separate bowl until they are thick and creamy and a ribbon-like trail forms when the whisks are lifted from the mixture. Fold in the flour and cardamom seeds, then pour the mixture into the prepared pan and bake in the oven for 12–15 minutes.

4 Dust a large sheet of wax paper with confectioners' sugar, then turn the cooked sponge out on to it. Trim the edges to neaten and roll from a short edge, leaving the wax paper in the roll. Set aside and leave to cool. When cool, unroll and spread the yogurt over the sponge, scatter the strawberries over the top and reroll the sponge without the wax paper. Dust with confectioners' sugar to serve.

FRESH FRUIT TARTLETS

These individual pastry cases, made with filo pastry, can be filled with a variety of delicious ingredients—here I have used plain soy yogurt flavored with orange rind and honey and topped with fresh summer fruits (see right). Fruit tartlets never fail to impress your guests and are ideal to serve at a summer tea party.

1 Preheat the oven to 375°F, 190°C, gas mark 5. To make the cases, cut the filo pastry into 32 squares. Cover with a damp cloth to prevent them from drying out. Gently press a square of the pastry into a 1¾-inch tartlet pan and sprinkle lightly with cinnamon. Lay a second square of pastry on top of the first, at an angle (so the pastry edge is ragged) and press gently into the pan. Set aside and repeat with the other tartlet tins until all the filo pastry is used up—you should have 16 pastry cases.

2 Bake the cases in the preheated oven for 5 minutes until the pastry is pale golden in color. Remove from the oven and leave to cool, then carefully remove the pastry cases from the tartlet pans and set aside.

3 To make the filling, beat the yogurt with the orange rind and honey in a bowl until well blended. Carefully spoon this mixture into the cooled pastry cases and arrange the summer fruits on top.

4 Place the red currant jelly in a small saucepan. Cook over low heat until it melts and becomes runny. Then gently brush the melted jelly over the fruits to glaze. Serve the tartlets cold.

2 ounces filo pastry, 4 sheets measuring approximately 12 x 16 inches

2–3 teaspoons ground cinnamon for sprinkling

¾ cup plain soy yogurt

Finely grated rind of 1 orange

2 teaspoons honey

1 pound summer fruits, such as raspberries, strawberries or blueberries

½ cup red currant jelly

Makes 16

MARZIPAN BAKLAVA

This lactose-free recipe is an adaptation of the Middle Eastern Baklava, a sweet dessert traditionally made of many layers of butter-drenched filo pastry, spices and chopped nuts.

Oil for greasing

13 ounces filo pastry, 24 sheets measuring approximately 12 x 16 inches

2 cups apple purée

11 ounces marzipan, chopped

½ cup honey

1 teaspoon ground cinnamon

Makes 15 pieces

1 Preheat the oven to 350°F, 180°C, gas mark 4. Lightly grease a 8 x 10-inch baking dish with oil. Place a sheet of filo pastry over the base of the baking dish and top with a little of the apple purée and chopped marzipan. Continue to layer the pastry, purée and marzipan in this way, finishing with a layer of pastry. Cover the remaining filo sheets with a damp cloth to prevent them from drying out. Score the top layer into squares or triangles and bake in the preheated oven for 45 minutes until golden.

2 A couple of minutes before removing the cooked Baklava from the oven, heat the honey in a saucepan with the cinnamon over low heat until runny. Remove the Baklava from the oven, drizzle the honey over the top and leave to stand for 5 minutes. Cut into triangles or squares to serve.

CINNAMON SWIRL TEA BREAD

Raisins are rolled into cinnamon dough to make a pleasing spiral pattern, which is revealed once the cooked loaf is sliced (see above).

4¾ cups all-purpose flour

1 tablespoon salt

1 tablespoon ground cinnamon

2 tablespoons vegetable shortening

3½ teaspoons (roughly 1½ packets)
active dry yeast

Oil for greasing

½ cup raisins

¼ cup packed light brown sugar

Makes 1¾ pound loaf

1 Sift the flour, salt and cinnamon into a bowl. Stir in the shortening and the yeast. Add 1¾ cup plus 2 tablespoons lukewarm water and mix to make a soft, not sticky dough. Turn out on to a floured surface and knead well for 10 minutes. Place the dough in an oiled bowl, then cover with greased plastic wrap. Leave in a warm place for 90 minutes until doubled in size.

2 Preheat the oven to 425°F, 220°C, gas mark 7. Grease a 2-pound loaf pan with oil. Knock back the dough and roll into a rectangle the same length as the pan but 3 times the width. Sprinkle over the raisins and roll up the dough from an edge that is the same length as the pan. Place into the pan and cover with oiled plastic wrap. Leave in a warm place for 30 minutes. Bake in the oven for 10 minutes; reduce the temperature to 190°F, 375°F, gas mark 5 and bake for 25–30 minutes. Turn out on to a wire rack to cool.

CITRUS RINGS WITH SUMMER BERRIES

A mixture of cherries, blackberries and raspberries is my choice of filling for these tasty citrus rings, but you can mix and match your own favorite summer fruit.

1 Grease 6 small 1⅓-cup ring molds (or savarin molds) with oil. To prepare the citrus rings, stir together the flour, salt, yeast and sugar in a mixing bowl until well blended. Gradually work in the eggs and 1⅓ cup hand-hot water. Then knead the dough on a floured work surface for 10 minutes.

2 Divide the dough into 6 portions, knead each one and shape into rounds. Using a floured finger, make a hole in the center of each round and place it in a greased ring mold. Cover the filled molds with greased plastic wrap and leave them in a warm place for 45 minutes until the dough doubles in size. Preheat the oven to 425°F, 220°C, gas mark 7.

3 Bake the bread rings in the preheated oven for 20 minutes until well risen and golden. Leave to cool in the molds for 5 minutes, then turn out on to a wire rack to cool completely.

4 Sift the confectioners' sugar into a bowl and gradually add the lemon juice. Beat the mixture until smooth, drizzle over the bread rings, then transfer them to serving plates. To make the filling, spoon the soy yogurt into the center of each bread ring. Divide the fruit into 6 portions and arrange a little of each portion on top of the yogurt and the remainder on the serving plate around the ring. Decorate each portion with the fresh mint or fruit leaves and sift a sprinkling of confectioners' sugar over each ring to serve.

FOR THE CITRUS RINGS

Oil for greasing

4¾ cups unbleached all-purpose flour

1 tablespoon salt

3½ teaspoons (roughly 1½ packets) active dry yeast

3 tablespoons superfine sugar

2 large eggs

1¾ cups confectioners' sugar

Juice of ½ lemon

FOR THE FILLING

⅔ cup plain soy yogurt

1 pound summer fruit, such as cherries, blackberries or raspberries

Fresh mint or fruit leaves to decorate

Confectioners' sugar for dusting

Serves 6

PEANUT BUTTER COOKIES

I could not believe my luck when I discovered that peanut butter is fantastic for making cookies in place of butter. These cookies keep fresh in an airtight container for four days or can be frozen for one month.

1 Preheat the oven to 375°F, 190°C, gas mark 5. Lightly grease 2 large baking sheets with oil. Beat together the peanut butter and yogurt in a mixing bowl. Add the sugar and mix well until all the ingredients are blended. Beat in the egg and gradually add the flour until the mixture is smooth.

2 Cover the cookie mixture and chill in the refrigerator for 15 minutes. Then shape the mixture into 25 walnut-sized balls using your hands and place on the baking sheets, leaving plenty of room between each cookie. Flatten each of these with a fork to a thickness of ½-inch. Bake in the preheated oven for 10–12 minutes, then leave to cool on a wire rack before serving.

Oil for greasing

⅔ cup crunchy peanut butter

3 tablespoons plain soy yogurt

¾ cup superfine sugar

1 large egg

1 cup and 1 tablespoon self-rising flour

Makes 25

SAVORY TOMATO SCONES

Oil for greasing

2¼ cups self-rising flour

1½ tablespoons tomato paste

½ cup plain soy yogurt, plus extra to serve

2 large eggs, beaten

Black and green olives, halved, 1 red and 1 yellow bell pepper, peeled and sliced thinly to serve

Makes 12

These savory scones are ideal for picnics—use them instead of bread with a selection of toppings, or simply eat them on their own.

1 Preheat the oven to 425°F, 220°C, gas mark 7. Lightly grease a large baking sheet with a little oil.

2 Sift the flour into a mixing bowl. Beat together the tomato paste, soy yogurt and eggs in a separate bowl until smooth. Pour this mixture into the flour and work to a soft, not sticky dough. Knead the dough on a floured surface, then roll it out to a thickness of ¾-inch. Use a 2-inch plain, circular biscuit cutter to cut scone shapes; reroll the trimmings as necessary.

3 Arrange the scones on the prepared baking sheet and bake in the oven for 12–15 minutes until golden and well risen. Serve warm, split and topped with soy yogurt, black and green olives and red and yellow bell peppers.

OLIVE SCONES

Omit the tomato paste and, instead, stir ¼ cup of pitted and chopped black or green olives into the flour. Stir in the yogurt and eggs as indicated above. Roll out the dough on a lightly floured work surface into a circular shape. Transfer to a baking sheet and mark into eight segments with the back of a knife. Bake in the preheated oven for 15–20 minutes until risen and golden. Serve the segments broken, with soups or cold meats and fish.

APRICOT SCONES

Oil for greasing

1½ cups self-rising flour

¼ cup superfine sugar

¾ cup dried apricots, chopped

½ cup plain soy yogurt, plus extra to serve

2 large eggs, beaten

Strawberry or raspberry preserves to serve

12 fresh strawberries to decorate

Makes 12

Traditionally, golden raisins or raisins are used to make sweet scones, but I love the flavor of scones with dried apricots (dried mango is also delicious). Top these scones with strawberry preserves, plain soy yogurt and fresh fruit for a tempting "cream" tea (see right).

1 Preheat the oven to 425°F, 220°C, gas mark 7. Lightly grease a large baking sheet with a little oil.

2 Sift the flour and sugar into a mixing bowl and stir in the apricots. Beat together the yogurt and eggs in a separate bowl until smooth. Pour this mixture into the flour and work to a soft, not sticky dough. Lightly knead the dough on a floured surface. Roll out the dough to a thickness of ¾-inch and use a 2-inch plain or fluted circular biscuit cutter to make scones— reroll the trimmings as necessary.

3 Arrange the scones on the baking sheet and bake in the preheated oven for 12–15 minutes until golden and well risen. Split and serve warm with fruit preserves and plain soy yogurt, topped with a fresh strawberry.

FOCACCIA

3 cups all-purpose flour

1 teaspoon salt

3½ teaspoons (roughly 1½ packets)
active dry yeast

½ cup extra virgin olive oil, plus
extra for greasing

3 tablespoons chopped fresh thyme

2 teaspoons coarse sea salt

Fresh thyme sprigs to serve

Makes 1 pound loaf

*This Italian bread (see below—on table) is made from pizza dough and
is baked in an oval shape, then drizzled with olive oil and herbs.*

1 Mix the flour, salt and yeast in a bowl. Add 3 tablespoons of the olive oil
and 1½ cups of lukewarm water. Stir to make a soft, not sticky dough.
Knead for 5 minutes on a lightly floured surface. Transfer to an oiled bowl,
cover with plastic wrap and leave in a warm place for 45 minutes until
doubled in size.

2 Preheat the oven to 400°F, 200°C, gas mark 6. Lightly grease a baking sheet
with olive oil. Turn out the dough on to a lightly floured surface and knead
in the thyme. Shape the dough into a large oval and place on the prepared
baking sheet. Using lightly floured fingers, press the dough to make
random dents in the surface. Cover with greased plastic wrap and leave in
a warm place for 30 minutes until doubled in size.

3 Remove the plastic wrap and bake the dough in the oven for 25 minutes
until golden and risen. Drizzle the remaining 3 tablespoons of olive oil
over the bread and scatter salt and thyme sprigs on top, then serve warm.

HERB BREAD ROLLS

Store-bought bread often contains dairy products, so it is better to make your own. These bread rolls (opposite—in basket) contain fresh herbs.

1   Sift the flour and salt into a bowl. Stir in the yeast, then 1¾ cups lukewarm water. Using a palette knife, then your hands, blend the mixture well. Turn out the dough on to a lightly floured surface, knead for 5 minutes until smooth and elastic, then place in an oiled bowl. Cover with greased plastic wrap and leave in a warm place for 45 minutes until doubled in size.

2   Preheat the oven to 400°F, 200°C, gas mark 6. Grease a baking sheet with oil. Turn out the dough on to a lightly floured surface, knead in the herbs, then shape into 12 even-sized ovals. Arrange them on the baking sheet. Cover with greased plastic wrap and leave for 30 minutes in a warm place until doubled in size. Sprinkle with flour and bake in the preheated oven for 20 minutes until the rolls sound hollow when tapped on the bases.

3 cups all-purpose flour, plus extra for sprinkling

1 teaspoon salt

3½ teaspoons (roughly 1½ packets) active dry yeast

Oil for greasing

3 tablespoons chopped fresh sage, parsley or thyme

Makes 12

POPPY SEED ROLLS

Omit the fresh herbs. Divide the dough into 14 portions and shape these into rounds. Arrange in 2 oiled 7-inch layer cake pans. Cover with greased plastic wrap and leave for 30 minutes in a warm place until the rolls are doubled in size and fill the pans. Sprinkle the rolls with poppy seeds and bake as above.

MALT LOAF

Fruity malt loaf is great at tea time—serve it warm or toast it and spread it with apricot conserve.

1   Melt the shortening, then mix the flours, yeast, salt, sugar and raisins in a bowl. Make a well in the center and pour in the shortening, malt extract, molasses and corn syrup. Stir, then, using your hands, knead the dough for 5 minutes until soft and sticky. Turn into a bowl and cover with greased plastic wrap. Leave in a warm place for 90 minutes until doubled in size.

2   Oil a 1-pound loaf pan. Knead the dough on a floured work surface until smooth. Place in the pan, cover with greased plastic wrap and leave in a warm place for 45 minutes. Preheat the oven to 375°F, 190°C, gas mark 5.

3   Bake the loaf in the oven for 45–50 minutes until well risen and cooked through. You may need to cover the loaf with wax paper during cooking to prevent the top from burning.

4   Heat the sugar and the water in a small saucepan over low heat until the sugar dissolves. Increase the heat and simmer for 2 minutes. Remove the loaf from the oven, immediately brush with the glaze and serve warm.

1⅔ cups wholewheat flour

1 cup all-purpose flour

3½ teaspoons (roughly 1½ packets) active dry yeast

Pinch each of salt and sugar

½ cup raisins

2 tablespoons vegetable shortening

1 tablespoon malt extract

1 teaspoon each molasses and dark corn syrup

Oil for greasing

3 tablespoons superfine sugar

3 tablespoons water

Makes 1 pound loaf

The nutritional information for each recipe refers to a single serving, unless otherwise stated. Optional ingredients are not included. The figures are intended as a guide only. If salt is given in a measured amount in the recipe it has been included in the analysis; if the recipe suggests adding a pinch of salt or seasoning to taste, salt has not been included.

p.10 French Onion Soup
233 Cal; 6g protein; 7g total fat; 1g saturated fat; 39g carbohydrate; 3g fiber; 357mg sodium; 96g calcium

p.10 Mixed Bean Soup
170–113 Cal; 8.5–6g protein; 6.5–4.5g total fat; 0.9–0.6g saturated fat; 20–13.5g carbohydrate; 8.6–6g fiber; 588–392mg sodium; 105–70mg calcium

p.11 Butternut Squash Soup
344 Cal; 6g protein; 17.5g total fat; 2.5g saturated fat; 44g carbohydrate; 5g fiber; 206mg sodium; 156mg calcium

p.12 Salmon & Saffron Risotto
373 Cal; 17g protein; 11g total fat; 2g saturated fat; 51g carbohydrate; 0.1g fiber; 28mg sodium; 27mg calcium

p.13 Lemon Thai Shrimp
163 Cal; 6g protein; 15g total fat; 2g saturated fat; 1g carbohydrate; 0.1g fiber; 1163mg sodium; 32mg calcium

p.13 Golden Scallops
107 Cal; 14g protein; 4.5g total fat; 1g saturated fat; 2.5g carbohydrate; 0.5g fiber; 136mg sodium; 53mg calcium

p.14 Chicken Satay
458 Cal; 40g protein; 31g total fat; 18g saturated fat; 5g carbohydrate; 1g fiber; 192mg sodium; 23mg calcium

p.14 Pheasant in Prosciutto
306 Cal; 33g protein; 17g total fat; 4g saturated fat; 5g carbohydrate; 1g fiber; 298mg sodium; 74mg calcium

p.16 Toasted Ciabatta Sandwich
725 Cal; 37g protein; 26g total fat; 4g saturated fat; 78g carbohydrate; 4.5g fiber; 1258mg sodium; 23mg calcium

p.16 Mini Pancakes with Bresaola & Arugula
219–146 Cal; 13–9g protein; 3.5–2.5g total fat; 0.7–0.5g saturated fat; 33–22g carbohydrate; 2–1g fiber; 851–567mg sodium; 133–88mg calcium

p.16 Roasted Vegetable Tarts
313 Cal; 7.5g protein; 16g total fat; 3g saturated fat; 36g carbohydrate; 4g fiber; 147mg sodium; 141mg calcium

p.18 Golden Asparagus with Lemon Pasta
237 Cal; 1.5g protein; 9.0g total fat; 1.5g saturated fat; 31.0g carbohydrate; 2g fiber; 7mg sodium; 16mg calcium

p.18 Mixed Bean Salad
96 Cal; 2g protein; 7.5g total fat; 1g saturated fat; 5.5g carbohydrate; 2g fiber; 114mg sodium; 21mg calcium

p.18 Grilled Endive
241 Cal; 5g protein; 23g total fat; 2g saturated fat; 5g carbohydrate; 2g fiber; 2mg sodium; 41mg calcium

p.19 Caesar Salad
450 Cal; 12g protein; 37g total fat; 5g saturated fat; 18g carbohydrate; 1g fiber; 791mg sodium; 151mg calcium

p.22 Warm Mackerel & Potato Salad
500 Cal; 20g protein; 43g total fat; 8g saturated fat; 8.5g carbohydrate; 1g fiber; 768mg sodium; 40mg calcium

p.22 Pan-fried Mackerel with Orange and Rosemary
540 Cal; 39g protein; 41g total fat; 8g saturated fat; 5g carbohydrate; 1g fiber; 263mg sodium; 76mg calcium

p.24 Smoked Cod with Bacon
477 Cal; 50g protein; 16g total fat; 3g saturated fat; 36g carbohydrate; 2.5g fiber; 2268mg sodium; 75mg calcium

p.24 Flounder with Peppers
290 Cal; 29g protein; 15g total fat; 2g saturated fat; 10g carbohydrate; 3.5g fiber; 192mg sodium; 97mg calcium

p.25 Crispy Hake & French Fries
863 Cal; 28.5g protein; 55g total fat; 12g saturated fat; 66g carbohydrate; 2.4g fiber; 610mg sodium; 45mg calcium

p.25 Potato-topped Fish Pie
722 Cal; 55g protein; 15.5g total fat; 3g saturated fat; 92g carbohydrate; 6g fiber; 1293mg sodium; 306mg calcium

p.27 Classic Kedgeree
391 Cal; 34g protein; 8g total fat; 2g saturated fat; 45g carbohydrate; 0g fiber; 940mg sodium; 70mg calcium

p.27 Salad Niçoise
616 Cal; 50g protein; 36g total fat; 6g saturated fat; 25g carbohydrate; 5g fiber; 1180mg sodium; 113mg calcium

p.28 Herb-coated Turkey
452 Cal; 28g protein; 4g total fat; 1g saturated fat; 80g carbohydrate; 1g fiber; 514mg sodium; 90mg calcium

**p.28/29 Topped Bruschetta:
with Roasted Vegetable Topping**
363 Cal; 4g protein; 29g total fat; 4g saturated fat; 24g carbohydrate; 1g fiber; 229mg sodium; 54mg calcium
with Duck Topping
350 Cal; 16.5g protein; 22g total fat; 3.5g saturated fat; 22g carbohydrate; 1g fiber; 287mg sodium; 60mg calcium

p.31 Crunchy Chicken Salad
400 Cal; 23g protein; 31g total fat; 5g saturated fat; 7g carbohydrate; 1g fiber; 324mg sodium; 37mg calcium

p.31 Chicken-stuffed Pitas
530 Cal; 29g protein; 18g total fat; 3g saturated fat; 66g carbohydrate; 4g fiber; 665mg sodium; 126mg calcium

p.32 Chinese-style Pork
204 Cal; 22g protein; 10g total fat; 2g saturated fat; 7g carbohydrate; 2.5g fiber; 424mg sodium; 45mg calcium

p.32 Spicy Beef
460 Cal; 37g protein; 29g total fat; 7.5g saturated fat; 7g carbohydrate; 1.5g fiber; 275mg sodium; 68mg calcium

p.33 Sausage & Bean Casserole
553 Cal; 22g protein; 45g total fat; 13g saturated fat; 15g carbohydrate; 4g fiber; 1961mg sodium; 53mg calcium

p.34 Seared Calf's Liver with Crispy Bacon
417 Cal; 27g protein; 34g total fat; 12g saturated fat; 2g carbohydrate; 0g fiber; 1019mg sodium; 11mg calcium

p.34 Lamb with Crispy Potatoes
319 Cal; 23g protein; 14g total fat; 5g saturated fat; 26g carbohydrate; 1.5g fiber; 84mg sodium; 30mg calcium

p.35 Bacon & Mushroom Omelette
377 Cal; 36g protein; 26g total fat; 7g saturated fat; 0.5g carbohydrate; 1.5g fiber; 1860mg sodium; 85mg calcium

p.36 Ratatouille Gratin
208 Cal; 5g protein; 12g total fat; 2g saturated fat; 21g carbohydrate; 4.5g fiber; 19mg sodium; 42mg calcium

p.37 Tabbouleh
270 Cal; 13g protein; 9g total fat; 2g saturated fat; 36g carbohydrate; 1.5g fiber; 535mg sodium; 43mg calcium

p.37 Spinach & Potato Curry
214 Cal; 8g protein; 7g total fat; 1g saturated fat; 31g carbohydrate; 6.5g fiber; 99mg sodium; 143mg calcium

p.38 Mushroom & Prosciutto Pizza
352 Cal; 14g protein; 17g total fat; 3g saturated fat; 38g carbohydrate; 3g fiber; 585mg sodium; 191mg calcium

p.38 Chunky Spanish Omelette
333 Cal; 16g protein; 22g total fat; 4.5g saturated fat; 19g carbohydrate; 4g fiber; 140mg sodium; 90mg calcium

p.42 Haddock with Beets
222 Cal; 31.5g protein; 7g total fat; 1g saturated fat; 10g carbohydrate; 2g fiber; 293mg sodium; 57mg calcium

p.42 Seared Tuna with Mixed Bean Salad
657 Cal; 62g protein; 29g total fat; 5g saturated fat; 38g carbohydrate; 13g fiber; 1050mg sodium; 186mg calcium

p.43 Warm Scallop & Avocado Salad
622 Cal; 34g protein; 51g total fat; 7g saturated fat; 7.5g carbohydrate; 4g fiber; 230mg sodium; 78mg calcium

p.44 Poached Salmon with Fresh Herb Dressing
330 Cal; 28g protein; 18g total fat; 3g saturated fat; 2.5g carbohydrate; 0.5g fiber; 157mg sodium; 58mg calcium

p.45 Roast Monkfish with Green Lentils
355 Cal; 45g protein; 5g total fat; 1g saturated fat; 36g carbohydrate; 8g fiber; 39mg sodium; 68mg calcium

p.45 Striped Mullet with Gooseberries
543 Cal; 80g protein; 18g total fat; 0.5g saturated fat; 13.5g carbohydrate; 2.0g fiber; 367mg sodium; 294mg calcium

p.46 Paella
450 Cal; 34g protein; 10g total fat; 2g saturated fat; 55g carbohydrate; 2.5g fiber; 261mg sodium; 94mg calcium

p.46 Fennel-stuffed Sea Bass
372 Cal; 55g protein; 12g total fat; 2g saturated fat; 1g carbohydrate; 1g fiber; 234mg sodium; 444mg calcium

p.48 Turkey with Preserved Lemons & Couscous
610 Cal; 65g protein; 15g total fat; 2.5g saturated fat; 48g carbohydrate; 1.5g fiber; 175mg sodium; 58mg calcium

p.49 Coq au Vin
500 Cal; 39g protein; 32g total fat; 10g saturated fat; 4.5g carbohydrate; 1g fiber; 764mg sodium; 29mg calcium

p.50 Thai Green Curry
550 Cal; 42g protein; 39g total fat; 31g saturated fat; 8g carbohydrate; 0g fiber; 422mg sodium; 32mg calcium

p.50 Turkey Tikka
236 Cal; 49g protein; 7g total fat; 1g saturated fat; 2g carbohydrate; 0g fiber; 314mg sodium; 35mg calcium

p.51 Pheasant Pie
991 Cal; 48g protein; 52g total fat; 11g saturated fat; 87g carbohydrate; 9g fiber; 532mg sodium; 220mg calcium

p.53 Cornish Game Hens with Sticky Glaze
560 Cal; 42g protein; 39g total fat; 10g saturated fat; 9g carbohydrate; 0.5g fiber; 153mg sodium; 25mg calcium

p.53 Duck with Cranberries
680 Cal; 35g protein; 53g total fat; 14g saturated fat; 16.5g carbohydrate; 2g fiber; 217mg sodium; 47mg calcium

p.54 Venison & Vegetable Pot Pies
330 Cal; 41g protein; 11g total fat; 3g saturated fat; 15.5g carbohydrate; 4g fiber; 140mg sodium; 66mg calcium

p.55 Beef Salad
280 Cal; 31g protein; 17g total fat; 4g saturated fat; 2.5g carbohydrate; 2g fiber; 86mg sodium; 75mg calcium

p.57 Lamb Tikka
813 Cal; 52g protein; 39g total fat; 20g saturated fat; 62g carbohydrate; 0g fiber; 277mg sodium; 57mg calcium

p.57 Roast Lamb with Shiitake Stuffing
285 Cal; 32g protein; 17g total fat; 6.5g saturated fat; 2g carbohydrate; 0.5g fiber; 109mg sodium; 29mg calcium

p.58 Lamb & Apricot Cobbler
675 Cal; 45g protein; 31g total fat; 8g saturated fat; 57g carbohydrate; 7g fiber; 540mg sodium; 253mg calcium

p.59 Fruity Pork Stew
366 Cal; 34g protein; 12g total fat; 3g saturated fat; 21g carbohydrate; 2.5g fiber; 127mg sodium; 49mg calcium

p.61 Vegetable Stir-fry
386 Cal; 12g protein; 10g total fat; 1g saturated fat; 65g carbohydrate; 6.5g fiber; 369mg sodium; 58mg calcium

p.64 Curried Sweet Potato
165 Cal; 1.5g protein; 8g total fat; 1g saturated fat; 24g carbohydrate; 3g fiber; 45mg sodium; 27mg calcium

p.65 Seared New Potatoes with Rosemary & Sea Salt
256–170 Cal; 4–2.5g protein; 12–8g total fat; 2–1g saturated fat; 36–24g carbohydrate; 2.5–1.5g fiber; 510–340mg sodium; 14–9mg calcium

p.65 Potato Cakes
205 Cal; 6g protein; 8g total fat; 1g saturated fat; 30g carbohydrate; 2.5g fiber; 75mg sodium; 31mg calcium

p.66 Perfect Baked Potatoes
183 Cal; 4g protein; 6g total fat; 1g saturated fat; 31g carbohydrate; 2.5g fiber; 13mg sodium; 10mg calcium

p.68 Zucchini with Bell Pepper, Garlic & Rosemary
106 Cal; 4.5g protein; 6.5g total fat; 1g saturated fat; 7g carbohydrate; 3g fiber; 4mg sodium; 60mg calcium

p.68 Orange-glazed Baby Carrots
45 Cal; 1g protein; 0.6g total fat; 0.1g saturated fat; 9g carbohydrate; 3g fiber; 52mg sodium; 45mg calcium

p.69 Pumpkin with Caraway Seeds
205 Cal; 1.5g protein; 17.5g total fat; 1g saturated fat; 10.5g carbohydrate; 2g fiber; 175mg sodium; 61mg calcium

p.69 Pattypan Risotto
378 Cal; 8.5g protein; 6.5g total fat; 1g saturated fat; 73g carbohydrate; 1g fiber; 2mg sodium; 59mg calcium

p.70 Mediterranean Stuffed Eggplant
70 Cal; 2.5g protein; 4g total fat; 1g saturated fat; 7.5g carbohydrate; 5g fiber; 11mg sodium; 33mg calcium

p.71 Gnocchi-topped Vegetables
470 Cal; 15g protein; 14g total fat; 2.5g saturated fat; 76g carbohydrate; 7g fiber; 1119mg sodium; 120mg calcium

p.72 Fennel & Snow Pea Stir-fry
105 Cal; 4g protein; 8g total fat; 1.5g saturated fat; 4.5g carbohydrate; 2g fiber; 580mg sodium; 31mg calcium

p.72 Vegetarian Stuffed Cabbage
180 Cal; 6g protein; 13g total fat; 1g saturated fat; 10.5g carbohydrate; 6g fiber; 10mg sodium; 101mg calcium

p.73 Red Cabbage with Pears
145 Cal; 2.5g protein; 3g total fat; 0.5g saturated fat; 29g carbohydrate; 4.5g fiber; 13mg sodium; 80mg calcium

p.75 Roast Tomatoes with Balsalmic Vinegar
150 Cal; 2g protein; 11.5g total fat; 2g saturated fat; 11g carbohydrate; 2.5g fiber; 19mg sodium; 20mg calcium

p.75 Triple Tomato & Avocado Salad
242 Cal; 2g protein; 22.5g total fat; 4g saturated fat; 8g carbohydrate; 3g fiber; 11mg sodium; 16mg calcium

p.76 Basic White Sauce
435 Cal; 13g protein; 29g total fat; 1.5g saturated fat; 31.5g carbohydrate; 0g fiber; 360mg sodium; 64mg calcium

p.76 Mayonnaise
(per 15ml) 80 Cal; 0.5g protein; 9g total fat; 1.2g saturated fat; 0g carbohydrate; 0g fiber; 6.3mg sodium; 2.5mg calcium

p.77 Tomato Sauce
590 Cal; 12g protein; 37g total fat; 16g saturated fat; 54g carbohydrate; 16g fiber; 209mg sodium; 132mg calcium

p.80 Avocado & Tuna Stuffed Tomato
360 Cal; 21g protein; 21.5g total fat; 4g saturated fat; 22g carbohydrate; 6g fiber; 368mg sodium; 48mg calcium

p.81 Tomato Catherine Wheels
13 Cal; 0.6g protein; 0.2g total fat; 0g saturated fat; 2g carbohydrate; 0.2g fiber; 13mg sodium; 3mg calcium

p.83 Fish Cakes with Tomato Salsa
195 Cal; 15g protein; 6g total fat; 1g saturated fat; 22g carbohydrate; 2g fiber; 198mg sodium; 44mg calcium

p.84 Chicken Fingers & French Fries
490 Cal; 22g protein; 33.5g total fat; 5g saturated fat; 26.5g carbohydrate; 1g fiber; 129mg sodium; 27mg calcium

p.85 Beef Meatballs with Gooey Centers
466 Cal; 39g protein; 30g total fat; 10g saturated fat; 11g carbohydrate; 2g fiber; 441mg sodium; 73mg calcium

p.85 Polenta-topped Pie
460 Cal; 41g protein; 20g total fat; 8g saturated fat; 28g carbohydrate; 2g fiber; 263mg sodium; 37mg calcium

p.86 Spaghetti Carbonara
415 Cal; 25g protein; 12g total fat; 3g saturated fat; 54g carbohydrate; 2.5g fiber; 1193mg sodium; 43mg calcium

p.86 Ham & Egg Packages
176 Cal; 12g protein; 4g total fat; 1g saturated fat; 20g carbohydrate;

0.5g fiber; 402mg sodium; 11mg calcium

p.88 Pork & Apple Burgers
330 Cal; 19g protein; 6g total fat; 1.5g saturated fat; 52g carbohydrate; 2g fiber; 557mg sodium; 119mg calcium

p.89 Pizza with Pork & Corn
340 Cal; 15.5g protein; 20g total fat; 5.5g saturated fat; 25g carbohydrate; 2.5g fiber; 458mg sodium; 151mg calcium

p.89 Honey Sausages & Mashed Potatoes
527 Cal; 13g protein; 27g total fat; 9.5g saturated fat; 62g carbohydrate; 3g fiber; 725mg sodium; 56mg calcium

p.90 Baked Marmalade Puddings
686 Cal; 9.5g protein; 35g total fat; 9g saturated fat; 86g carbohydrate; 1g fiber; 362mg sodium; 176mg calcium

p.91 Chocolate Bread Pudding
405 Cal; 7g protein; 20g total fat; 6.5g saturated fat; 51.5g carbohydrate; 1g fiber; 301mg sodium; 70mg calcium

p.91 Oat Bars
245 Cal; 3.5g protein; 13g total fat; 3g saturated fat; 30.5g carbohydrate; 2g fiber; 101mg sodium; 25mg calcium

p.93 Mini Plum Crisps
335 Cal; 3.5g protein; 11g total fat; 3g saturated fat; 60g carbohydrate; 2.5g fiber; 113mg sodium; 66mg calcium

p.93 Fruity Milk Shakes
220 Cal; 12g protein; 8g total fat; 1.5g saturated fat; 27g carbohydrate; 3g fiber; 46mg sodium; 48mg calcium

p.93 Chocolate Chip Mini Muffins
100 Cal; 1g protein; 6.5g total fat; 2g saturated fat; 10g carbohydrate; 0.5g fiber; 89mg sodium; 27mg calcium

p.96 Bluebery Rice Pudding
528 Cal; 2g protein; 41g total fat; 32g saturated fat; 19g carbohydrate; 1g fiber; 34mg sodium; 45mg calcium

p.97 Baked Chocolate Pudding
637 Cal; 11g protein; 33g total fat; 14g saturated fat; 80g carbohydrate; 2g fiber; 322mg sodium; 69mg calcium

p.97 Baked Mini Pineapples
326 Cal; 4g protein; 0.5g total fat; 0.1g saturated fat; 80g carbohydrate; 4.5g fiber; 55mg sodium; 58mg calcium

p.98 Hot Fruit Soufflé with Sloe Gin-Macerated Fruits
300 Cal; 6g protein; 8.5g total fat; 2.5g saturated fat; 49g carbohydrate; 1.5g fiber; 155mg sodium; 52mg calcium

p.98 Hot Coffee Soufflé
210 Cal; 9g protein; 12g total fat; 3.5g saturated fat; 16g carbohydrate; 1g fiber; 145mg sodium; 44mg calcium

p.99 Souffléed Omelette with Caramelized Orchard Fruits
350 Cal; 12.5g protein; 10g total fat; 3g saturated fat; 59g carbohydrate; 6g fiber; 141mg sodium; 78mg calcium

p.99 Blueberry Clafoutis
235 Cal; 11g protein; 10.5g total fat; 3g saturated fat; 26g carbohydrate; 1g fiber; 131mg sodium; 76mg calcium

p.101 Crème Brûlée
200 Cal; 5g protein; 3.5g total fat; 0.5g saturated fat; 40g carbohydrate; 1g fiber; 1mg sodium; 10mg calcium

p.101 Toffee Bananas
365 Cal; 2g protein; 15g total fat; 2g saturated fat; 56g carbohydrate; 1g fiber; 26mg sodium; 47mg calcium

p.102 Warm Spiced Fruit Compote
228 Cal; 2.5g protein; 0.5g total fat; 0.1g saturated fat; 50g carbohydrate; 7g fiber; 20mg sodium; 42mg calcium

p.102 Poached Pears
227 Cal; 0.5g protein; 0.2g total fat; 0g saturated fat; 49g carbohydrate; 3.5g fiber; 12mg sodium; 25mg calcium

p.103 Fresh Fruit Terrine
90–68 Cal; 6–4.5g protein; 0.5–0.4g total fat; 0.2–0.1g saturated fat; 17–12.5g carbohydrate; 4–3g fiber; 28–21mg sodium; 59–45mg calcium

p.103 Upside-down Fruit Tart
427 Cal; 6.5g protein; 16g total fat; 3.5g saturated fat; 68g carbohydrate; 1g fiber; 270mg sodium; 138mg calcium

p.104 Individual Summer Puddings
253 Cal; 6g protein; 1g total fat; 0.2g saturated fat; 58g carbohydrate; 2.5g fiber; 290mg sodium; 84mg calcium

p.104 Orchard Strudel
223 Cal; 3g protein; 0.6g total fat; 0g saturated fat; 54g carbohydrate; 3g fiber; 3mg sodium; 12mg calcium

p.107 Raspberry Ice Meringue Nest
228 Cal; 6g protein; 4.5g total fat; 1g saturated fat; 44g carbohydrate; 1g fiber; 41mg sodium; 25mg calcium

p.108 Mango Sorbet
56 Cal; 1.5g protein; 0g total fat; 0g saturated fat; 13.5g carbohydrate; 0.5g fiber; 25mg sodium; 10mg calcium

p.108 Strawberry Granita
102 Cal; 0.7g protein; 0g total fat; 0g saturated fat; 12g carbohydrate; 1g fiber; 14mg sodium; 21mg calcium

p.109 Coconut Ice Cream with Curried Fruit Salad
500 Cal; 6g protein; 31g total fat; 22g saturated fat; 37g carbohydrate; 2g fiber; 60mg sodium; 47mg calcium

p.112 Chestnut Log
251 Cal; 7g protein; 7.5g total fat; 3g saturated fat; 41g carbohydrate; 0.5g fiber; 45mg sodium; 42mg calcium

p.112 Spicy Syrup Cake
485 Cal; 7g protein; 21g total fat; 6g saturated fat; 72g carbohydrate; 1.5g fiber; 372mg sodium; 183mg calcium

p.113 Carrot Cake
270 Cal; 7g protein; 3g total fat; 1g saturated fat; 58g carbohydrate; 2g fiber; 239mg sodium; 169mg calcium

p.115 Chocolate Cake Bars
210 Cal; 3.5g protein; 10.5g total fat; 2g saturated fat; 27g carbohydrate; 1g fiber; 126mg sodium; 84mg calcium

p.115 Mocha Bars
160 Cal; 3g protein; 3.5g total fat; 1.5g saturated fat; 31g carbohydrate; 1g fiber; 27mg sodium; 25mg calcium

p.116 Simple Fruit Cake
600 Cal; 7g protein; 21g total fat; 6g saturated fat; 104g carbohydrate; 2.5g fiber; 356mg sodium; 155mg calcium

p.116 Strawberry & Cardamom Roll
170 Cal; 6.5g protein; 4.5g total fat; 1g saturated fat; 28g carbohydrate; 0.5g fiber; 44mg sodium; 40mg calcium

p.117 Fresh Fruit Tartlets
50 Cal; 1.5g protein; 0.5g total fat; 0.1g saturated fat; 10g carbohydrate; 0.8g fiber; 2mg sodium; 8mg calcium

p.117 Marzipan Baklava
218 Cal; 4.5g protein; 6g total fat; 0.5g saturated fat; 37.5g carbohydrate; 1.5g fiber; 5mg sodium; 25 mg calcium

p.118 Cinnamon Swirl Tea Bread
(whole loaf) 2975 Cal; 70g protein; 30g total fat; 5g saturated fat; 649g carbohydrate; 23g fiber; 6196mg sodium; 1037mg calcium

p.119 Citrus Rings with Summer Berries
592 Cal; 16g protein; 5g total fat; 1g saturated fat; 130g carbohydrate; 4g fiber; 1023mg sodium; 185mg calcium

p.119 Peanut Butter Cookies
92 Cal; 2.5g protein; 4g total fat; 1g saturated fat; 12g carbohydrate; 0.5g fiber; 50mg sodium; 25mg calcium

p.120 Savory Tomato Scones
105 Cal; 4g protein; 2g total fat; 0.5g saturated fat; 19.5g carbohydrate; 1g fiber; 107mg sodium; 94mg calcium

p.120 Apricot Scones
105 Cal; 3.5g protein; 2g total fat; 0.5g saturated fat; 20g carbohydrate; 1g fiber; 75mg sodium; 70mg calcium

p.122 Focaccia
(whole loaf) 2048 Cal; 46g protein; 61g total fat; 8.5g saturated fat; 350g carbohydrate; 14g fiber; 5914mg sodium; 640mg calcium

p.123 Herb Bread Rolls
129 Cal; 4g protein; 0.5g total fat; 0.1g saturated fat; 29g carbohydrate; 1g fiber; 165mg sodium; 53mg calcium

p.123 Malt Loaf
(whole loaf) 1802 Cal; 49g protein; 27.5g total fat; 5g saturated fat; 363g carbohydrate; 26g fiber; 1116 mg sodium; 396mg calcium

Index

ACKNOWLEDGMENTS

Carroll & Brown would
particularly like to thank Jane
Zukin for her expert advice and
invaluable comments on the
manuscript. We would also like
to thank Victoria Spencer for so
carefully Americanizing the
recipes.

Food preparation: Lucy Knox
and Sarah Lowman
Art Director: Chrissie Lloyd
Nutritional analysis: Fiona
Hunter

Thanks also to Laura Price,
Sandra Brooke, Dawn
Henderson and Charlotte Beech
for their assistance.